Snapshots

A collection of short stories

Compiled by G U Y D U N B A R

CAMBRIDGE
UNIVERSITY PRESS

CAMBRIDGE UNIVERSITY PRESS
Cambridge, New York, Melbourne, Madrid, Cape Town, Singapore,
São Paulo, Delhi, Dubai, Tokyo, Mexico City

Cambridge University Press
The Edinburgh Building, Cambridge CB2 8RU, UK

www.cambridge.org
Information on this title: www.cambridge.org/9780521485272

First published 1995
14th printing 2010

Printed in the United Kingdom at the University Press, Cambridge

A catalogue record for this publication is available from the British Library

ISBN 978-0-521-48527-2 Paperback

VN

Contents

Introduction

Short stories offer similar experiences and pleasure to novels. They enable pupils to come into contact with a wide range of literary contexts. Through these, pupils can recognise their own thoughts, feelings and ideas – and be helped to make sense of them. At the same time, short stories introduce pupils to experiences, attitudes and values outside their own personal circumstances, and offer them opportunities to reflect on and evaluate these.

Thus, they provide a wide range of shared experience and, through this, common reference points on which later work can draw. In doing so, short stories make a valuable contribution to pupils' increasing grasp of literary form and language – the elements of character/relationship, atmosphere, setting, structure and language all being focused in manageable ways.

In addition, while short stories tend to focus on a moment, a single incident or experience, the best do so in order to illuminate wider matters.

This collection has been designed to enable pupils to experience a wide variety of:

- styles of writing
- situations
- characters
- relationships
- emotions
- issues.

They have been selected according to an explicit set of criteria:

- quality/vigour of language
- imaginative energy
- narrative drive

- accessibility to pupils
- popularity with pupils.

Most of the stories have been written very recently. Most, but not all, focus on the experiences of characters in the age-range of the intended auidence. Both men and women writers are represented.

All the stories can be read to, by, or with pupils at Key Stage 3 in no more than about 15 minutes. They are all good for reading aloud.

The order in which they appear here has arisen from classroom practice as a regular component of normal English work. Generally speaking:

- the first third of the stories have been used with Year 7;
- the middle third with Year 8;
- and the last third with Year 9.

Used in this way, they provide a comprehensive introduction to the short story form.

However, because there is always variety in reading experience and ability within classes, and because there is also variety in reading interest, the stories can also be targeted at particular groups within a class. That is, different groups within the same class can work on different stories at the same time. This collection and the follow-up work which accompanies it offer a wide range of opportunities to pupils across the ability range.

In general terms, the main purposes of *Snapshots* and the related work in *Developing Snapshots* are:

- to enable a developing understanding of and response to stories;
- to promote the purposeful use of language in both speech and writing;
- to provide structures within which the skills of speaking, listening, reading and writing work together;
- to help pupils' developing awareness of personal, social and moral issues;
- to provide opportunities for pupils to consider common

personal experiences – and also those which lie beyond their own personal experience.

Consequently, these stories, supported by the follow-up activities in *Developing Snapshots*, provide springboards for both 'language' and 'literature' work, and thus help pupils develop the skills required for GCSE/Key Stage 4.

GUY DUNBAR

The Pudding Like a Night on the Sea

ANN CAMERON

'I'M GOING TO make something special for your mother,' my father said.

My mother was out shopping. My father was in the kitchen looking at the pots and the pans and the jars of this and that.

'What are you going to make?' I said.

'A pudding,' he said.

My father is a big man with wild black hair. When he laughs, the sun laughs in the window-panes. When he thinks, you can almost see his thoughts sitting on all the tables and chairs. When he is angry, me and my little brother Huey shiver to the bottom of our shoes.

'What kind of pudding will you make?' Huey said.

'A wonderful pudding,' my father said. 'It will taste like a whole raft of lemons. It will taste like a night on the sea.'

Then he took down a knife and sliced five lemons in half. He squeezed the first one. Juice squirted in my eye.

'Stand back!' he said, and squeezed again. The seeds flew out on the floor. 'Pick up those seeds, Huey!' he said.

Huey took the broom and swept them up.

My father cracked some eggs and put the yolks in a pan and the whites in a bowl. He rolled up his sleeves and pushed back his hair and beat up the yolks. 'Sugar, Julian!' he said, and I poured in the sugar.

He went on beating. Then he put in lemon juice and cream and set the pan on the stove. The pudding bubbled and he stirred it fast. Cream splashed on the stove.

'Wipe that up, Huey!' he said.

Huey did.

It was hot by the stove. My father loosened his collar and pushed at his sleeves. The stuff in the pan was getting thicker and thicker. He held the beater up high in the air. 'Just right!' he said, and sniffed in the smell of the pudding.

He whipped the egg whites and mixed them into the pudding. The pudding looked softer and lighter than air.

'Done!' he said. He washed all the pots, splashing water on the floor, and wiped the counter so fast his hair made circles around his head.

'Perfect!' he said. 'Now I'm going to take a nap. If something important happens, bother me. If nothing important happens, don't bother me. And – the pudding is for your mother. Leave the pudding alone!'

He went to the living room and was asleep in a minute, sitting straight up in his chair.

Huey and I guarded the pudding.

'Oh, it's a wonderful pudding,' Huey said.

'With waves on the top like the ocean,' I said.

'I wonder how it tastes,' Huey said.

'Leave the pudding alone,' I said.

'If I just put my finger in – there – I'll know how it tastes,' Huey said.

And he did it.

'You did it!' I said. 'How does it taste?'

'It tastes like a whole raft of lemons,' he said. 'It tastes like a night on the sea.'

'You've made a hole in the pudding!' I said. 'But since you did it, I'll have a taste.' And it tasted like a whole night of lemons. It tasted like floating at sea.

'It's such a big pudding,' Huey said. 'It can't hurt to have a little more.'

'Since you took more, I'll have more,' I said.

'That was a bigger lick than I took!' Huey said. 'I'm going to have more again.'

'Whoops!' I said.

'You put in your whole hand!' Huey said. 'Look at the pudding you spilled on the floor!'

'I am going to clean it up,' I said. And I took the rag from the sink.

'That's not really clean,' Huey said.

'It's the best I can do,' I said.

'Look at the pudding!' Huey said.

It looked like craters on the moon. 'We have to smooth this over,' I said. 'So it looks the way it did before! Let's get spoons.'

And we evened the top of the pudding with spoons, and while we evened it, we ate some more.

'There isn't much left,' I said.

'We were supposed to leave the pudding alone,' Huey said.

'We'd better get away from here,' I said. We ran into our bedroom and crawled under the bed. After a long time we heard my father's voice.

'Come into the kitchen, dear,' he said. 'I have something for you.'

'Why, what is it?' my mother said, out in the kitchen.

Under the bed, Huey and I pressed ourselves to the wall.

'Look,' said my father, out in the kitchen. 'A wonderful pudding.'

'Where is the pudding?' my mother said.

'WHERE ARE YOU BOYS?' my father said. His voice went through every crack and corner of the house.

We felt like two leaves in a storm.

'WHERE ARE YOU? I SAID!' My father's voice was booming.

Huey whispered to me, 'I'm scared.'

We heard my father walking slowly through the rooms.

'Huey!' he called. 'Julian!'

We could see his feet. He was coming into our room.

He lifted the bedspread. There was his face, and his eyes like black lightning. He grabbed us by the legs and pulled.

'STAND UP!' he said.

We stood.

'What do you have to tell me?' he said.

'We went outside,' Huey said, 'and when we came back, the pudding was gone!'

'Then why were you hiding under the bed?' my father said.

We didn't say anything. We looked at the floor.

'I can tell you one thing,' he said. 'There is going to be some beating here now! There is going to be some whipping!'

The curtains at the window were shaking. Huey was holding my hand.

'Go into the kitchen!' my father said. 'Right now!'

We went into the kitchen.

'Come here, Huey!' my father said.

Huey walked towards him, his hands behind his back.

'See these eggs?' my father said. He cracked them and put the yolks in a pan and set the pan on the counter. He stood a chair by the counter. 'Stand up here,' he said to Huey.

Huey stood on the chair by the counter.

'Now it's time for your beating!' my father said.

Huey started to cry. His tears fell in with the egg yolks.

'Take this!' my father said. My father handed him the egg beater. 'Now beat those eggs,' he said. 'I want this to be a good beating!'

'Oh!' Huey said. He stopped crying. And he beat the egg yolks.

'Now you, Julian, stand here!' my father said.

I stood on a chair by the table.

'I hope you're ready for your whipping!'

I didn't answer. I was afraid to say yes or no.

'Here!' he said, and he set the egg whites in front of me. 'I want these whipped and whipped well!'

'Yes, sir!' I said, and started whipping.

My father watched us. My mother came into the kitchen and watched us.

After a while Huey said, 'This is hard work.'

'That's too bad,' my father said. 'Your beating's not done!' And he added sugar and cream and lemon juice to Huey's pan and put the pan on the stove. And Huey went on beating.

'My arm hurts from whipping,' I said.

'That's too bad,' my father said. 'Your whipping's not done.'

So I whipped and whipped, and Huey beat and beat.

'Hold that beater in the air, Huey!' my father said.

Huey held it in the air.

'See!' my father said. 'A good pudding stays on the beater. It's thick enough now. Your beating's done.' Then he turned to me. 'Let's see those egg whites, Julian!' he said. They were puffed up and fluffy. 'Congratulations, Julian!' he said. 'Your whipping's done.'

He mixed the egg whites into the pudding himself. Then he passed the pudding to my mother.

'A wonderful pudding,' she said. 'Would you like some, boys?'

'No thank you,' we said.

She picked up a spoon. 'Why, this tastes like a whole raft of lemons,' she said. 'This tastes like a night on the sea.'

Boys Will Be Boys

WENDY EDMOND

MUM PUTS DOWN her knife and fork.

'They're at it again,' she says.

The cars on the road are a distant whoosh, whoosh. It's the beginning of a hot Sunday afternoon. Mum and us kids are eating lunch. Dad is out working somewhere.

'Quick, close the windows. I don't know, I slave away in this house every day. Not that anyone seems to notice. It's all work and no pay, that's what. Just get the place clean and then those townies come out here and raise a dust-storm. Why can't the council seal the road? Your father's been on at them for years. Close the windows before the dust gets in.'

We run from room to room closing all the windows. From the front of the house we can see the townies' cars passing our gate. Dust rolls towards us as each car passes. Whoosh, whoosh.

Back in the kitchen it's hot now the windows are closed. We hurry through the meal, longing to get outside.

'If you kids think you're going to rush off and play, you've got another think coming. Your father hasn't had his meal yet. You three can go and help him finish his work. And you,' she turns to me, 'it's your turn to do the dishes. I've got work to do.'

The others go off to find Dad. Will I never get outside? 'Aw gee, Mum, Chris is coming soon. We're going to play in the trees.'

'Not before the dishes are done. Chris can help too.'

Chris doesn't turn up in time to help. I do them and wander outside. What a relief! It's so hot in there.

'Gidday, Nicky.' Chris comes cycling up the drive.

'Hi. Let's get going before the others have finished helping Dad.'

We leave the bike against the house and head for the trees. Quickly we climb to our platform looking over the dusty gravel road. These macrocarpa trees fell down in a storm last year. They kept on growing and now their great leafy branches provide us with forts, hiding-places, stages, slides, and platforms.

This one is the best. Chris and I come here every Sunday afternoon. Immediately below us the townies are driving their cars. One after another they head towards the beach. Whoosh, whoosh. The dust from the road rises in choking clouds with each car. We'll get our own back.

'We'll have to hurry, Chris. Come over here. I found some branches loaded with nuts yesterday. I dumped them over here.'

We rip the nuts from the macrocarpa branches, piling them on the platform where we can grab them easily.

'How's your throwing arm, Nicky? Reckon we'll get more than last week?'

'Too right we will. I reckon we get more every week, don't we? And they'll all have their windows open today. It's so hot.'

We look down at the cars. Sure enough, all the drivers have their windows open. Their elbows jut out from the cars as they drive along with one hand on the wheel. Each car contains a family. Mum and Dad are in the front, kids in the back. Everyone has their swimming-togs on, ready for the beach.

'Gee, I wish we were going to the beach, too.'

'I don't know. We can have just as much fun up here I reckon.'

We settle down to throwing nuts at the cars. The idea is to get a nut into a driver's lap. The one who gets the most nuts through the car window and onto the lap wins. We never get all that many through. The cars go too fast. But it's fun.

'You remember that guy last week? He didn't know what had happened to him. I bet those townies don't know a macrocarpa nut when they see one. And they never think to look up here.'

We're throwing away all the time but we don't seem too good at it today. The cars are going faster than usual. The dust gets heavier and heavier in the air. We throw harder and harder.

'If we don't get one soon, I'm going off to find some nests. It's getting boring.'

'Aw, come off it, Chris. We just have to warm up, that's all.'

'I'm warm enough. Don't tell me you aren't getting sick of it. I mean if we could get just one I'd be happy. Just one.'

'Well, you're not going to get one if you stop throwing. Come on, try a few more. If it doesn't work then we'll go and do something else.'

'Okay.'

There's a car beneath us going a bit slower than the others. All its windows are open. With all our might we both hurl our nuts.

'Missed again. Come on, Nicky. Let's go and find something else to do. I want to get at those nests we saw last week.'

Just then we hear a man shouting. The car has stopped. The townie has got out. He's coming down the road, shouting.

'We hit him!'

'Ssshhh . . . lie still.' We both freeze.

'I'll get you. You wait till I find you. I'll thrash the living daylights out of you.'

'We'd better move. He'll see us up here.'

'Okay, but don't make a sound. You go that way and I'll go down here. Don't break any branches, he'll hear us.'

We skedaddle, plunging down through the mess of branches and trunks, trying to get to the ground where we can hide in safety. I hit the ground first, right next door to a rotting dead sheep. Chris lands on top of me.

'Pooh! What a smell! Let's get out of here.'

'Ssshhh. He's just through there.'

'All right, I know you're in there. Come on out you little devils. If you don't come out before I've counted ten I'm coming in to get you. Then you'll be sorry. I know you're in there. One, two, three . . .'

We crouch down and start running silently up the length of the trees. If we can get up the end, over the gate, through the hedge, and up the drive, we'll be safe. Ssshhh. We run.

'. . . eight, nine, ten. I'm coming in. And when I get you boys I'll tan your hides.'

We reach the gate. It's hidden from the man's view. I get to the top and fall off into the ditch, tearing my jersey and cutting my elbow. I push my sleeves up so Mum won't notice the hole at tea-time.

'Come on, Nicky. Don't be so clumsy.'

'All right, you brats. Don't think I won't find you. And when I do . . . Your father's going to hear about this.'

Through the hedge we creep and out onto the drive. I want to go back to the house. Chris wants to have a look at the man. 'It's all right. He won't guess it was us. He thinks we're still in the trees, hiding.'

'Okay, but you're responsible. I don't want to get a hiding.'

We walk down the drive, straightening our clothes and hair. Just as we get to the gate, the man comes up. He's very red in the face. His wife and kids are starting to shout, too.

'Come on, Dad. We want to get to the beach. Forget about it.'

He stops. We wait. I wish we were back at the house.

'You kids live here, do you? Seen any boys around? They've been throwing things at my car. They're down in those trees somewhere.'

'Boys? There were some staying on the farm next door. Could have been them. They sometimes play in those trees.'

'Well, next time you see them, you tell them from me that they'd better cut it out. I'm not going to stand for it. For two pins I'd go and see their father.'

'Come on, Dad. We want to get to the beach. It's late.'

'They're only visitors. Their father isn't there.'

'Well, you tell them to cut it out. And if it happens again . . .'

The townie strides over to his car and gets in. He slams the door and drives away. The dust rises behind him. Chris and I look at each other and burst out laughing.

'What are you two doing? It's time to get the tea ready. Who was that man?' Mum comes down the drive, wiping her hands on her apron.

'I don't know, you're never around when I need you. Get inside and make some tea. Dad'll be needing it soon.'

'We've only been playing in the trees.'

'Playing in the trees. What you girls find to do down there all afternoon beats me. And no doubt you've torn your clothes as usual, Nicky. You'd earn your keep more if you did what I told you. Now go and make the tea. And keep the windows closed. I'm not going to dust that house again.'

Equal Rights

BERNARD ASHLEY

'CAN'T YOU READ?'

The man was looking at me and reaching under his counter as if he were going for his gun. He came up with another of his signs to spread over the front of a paper.

'Only two children at a time allowed in this shop,' he read out loudly.

I looked across at the two kids in the corner. They were pretending to pick Penny Chews while they gawped at the girls in the magazines. OK, I made three, but I wasn't there for the same reason as them. Couldn't he recognise business when he saw it?

'I'm not buying,' I said, 'I've come about the job.'

He frowned at me, in between watching the boys in the corner. 'What job?' he said. He was all on edge with three of us in the shop.

' ''Reliable paperboy wanted'',' I told him. ' ''Enquire within.'' It's in the window. I'm enquiring within.'

'Hurry up, you two!' he shouted. And then he frowned at me again as if I was something from outer space.

' ''Reliable paperboy required'', that says. If I'd meant boy or girl I'd have put it on, wouldn't I? Or ''paperperson''!' He did this false laugh for the benefit of a man with a briefcase standing at the counter.

'Oh,' I said, disappointed. 'Only I'm reliable, that's all. I get up early with my dad, I'm never off school, and I can tell the difference between the Sun and the Beano.'

'I'm glad someone can,' the man with the briefcase said.

But the paper man didn't laugh. He was looking at me, hard.

'Where do you live?' he asked.

'Round the corner.'

'Could you start at seven?'

'Six, if you like.'

'Rain or shine, winter and summer?'

'No problem.' I stared at him, and he stared at me. He looked as if he was trying to decide whether or not to give women the vote.

'All right,' he said, 'I'll give you a chance. Start Monday. Seven o'clock, do your own marking up. Four pounds a week, plus Christmas tips. Two weeks holiday without pay . . .'

Now that he'd made up his mind he smiled at me, over-doing the big favour.

'Is that what the boys get?' I asked. 'Four pounds a week?'

He started unwrapping a packet of fags. 'I don't see how that concerns you. The money suits or it doesn't. Four pounds is what I said and four pounds is what I meant. Take it or leave it.' He looked at Briefcase again, shaking his head at the cheek of the girl.

I walked back to the door. 'I'll leave it, then,' I said, 'seeing the boys get five pounds, and a week's holiday with pay.' I knew all this because Jason used to do it. 'Thanks anyway, I'll tell my dad what you said . . .'

I slammed out of the shop. I was mad, I can tell you. Cheap labour, he was after; thought he was on to a good thing for a minute, you could tell that.

The trouble was, I really needed a bit of money coming in, saving for those shoes and things I wanted. There was no way I'd get them otherwise. But I wasn't going to be treated any different from the boys. I wouldn't have a shorter round or lighter papers, would I? Everything'd be the same, except the money.

I walked the long way home, thinking. It was nowhere near Guy Fawkes and Carol Singing was even further away. So that really only left car washing – and they leave the rain to wash the cars round our way.

Hearing this baby cry gave me the idea. Without thinking about it, I knocked at the door where the bawling was coming from.

The lady opened it and stared at me like you stare at double-glazing salesmen, when you're cross for being brought to the door.

' "Baby-play calling", ' I said – making up the name from somewhere.

The lady said, 'Eh?' and she looked behind me to see who was pulling my strings.

' "Baby-play", ' I said. 'We come and play with your baby in your own home. Keep it happy. Or walk it out – not going across main roads.'

She opened the door a bit wider. The baby crying got louder.

'How much?' she asked.

That really surprised me. I'd felt sorry about calling from the first lift of the knocker, and here she was taking me seriously.

'I don't know,' I said. 'Whatever you think . . .'

'Well . . .' She looked at me to see if she'd seen me before; to see if I was local enough to be trusted. Then I was glad I had the high school jumper on, so she knew I could be traced. 'You push Bobby down the shops and get Mr Dawson's magazines, and I'll give you twenty pence. Take your time, mind.'

'All right,' I said. 'Thank you very much.'

She got this little push-chair out, and the baby came as good as gold – put its foot in the wheel a couple of times and nearly twisted its head off trying to see who I was, but I kept up the talking, and I stopped while it stared at a cat, so there wasn't any fuss.

When I got to the paper shop I took Bobby in with me.

'Afternoon,' I said, trying not to make too much of coming back. 'We've come down for Mr Dawson's papers, haven't we, Bobby?'

You should have seen the man's face.

'Mr Dawson's?' he asked, burning his finger on a match. 'Number 29?'

'Yes, please.'

'Are you . . .?' He nodded at Bobby and then at me as if he was making some link between us.

'That's right,' I said.

He fumbled at a pile behind him and lifted out the magazines. He laid them on the counter.

'Dawson' it said on the top. I looked at the titles to see what Mr Dawson enjoyed reading.

Worker's Rights was one of them. And *Trade Union Times* was the other. They had pictures on their fronts. One had two men pulling together on a rope. The other had a woman bus driver waving out of her little window. They told you the sort of man Mr Dawson was – one of those trade union people you get on television kicking up a fuss over wages, or getting cross when women are treated different to men. Just the sort of bloke I could do with on my side, I thought.

'Oh, look,' he said, with a green grin. 'I've got last month's *Pop Today* left over. You can have it if you like, with my compliments . . .'

'Thanks a lot,' I said. Now I saw the link in his mind. He thought I was Mr Dawson's daughter. He thought there'd be all sorts of trouble now, over me being offered lower wages than the boys.

'And about that job. Stupid of me, I'd got it wrong. What did I say – four pounds a week?'

'I think so,' I said. 'It sounded like four.'

'How daft can you get? It was those kids in the corner. Took my attention off. Of course it's five, you realise that. Have you spoken to your dad yet?'

'No, not yet.'

He stopped leaning so hard on the counter. 'Are you still interested?'

'Yes. Thank you very much.'

He came round the front and shook hands with me. 'Monday at

seven,' he said. 'Don't be late . . .' But you could tell he was only saying it, pretending to be the big boss.

'Right.' I turned the push-chair round. 'Say ta-ta to the man, Bobby,' I said.

Bobby just stared, like at the cat.

The paper man leaned over. 'Dear little chap,' he said.

'Yeah, smashing. But Bobby's a girl, not a chap, aren't you Bobby? At least, that's what Mrs Dawson just told me.'

I went out of the shop, while my new boss made this gurgling sound and knocked a pile of papers on the floor.

He'd made a show-up of himself, found out too late that I wasn't Mr Dawson's daughter.

I ran and laughed and zig-zagged Bobby along the pavement. 'Good for us! Equal rights, eh, Bobby? Equal rights!'

But Bobby's mind was all on the ride. She couldn't care less what I was shouting. All she wanted was someone to push her fast, to feel the wind on her face. Boy or girl, it was all the same to her.

M13 on Form

GENE KEMP

Told by X who never dares to give his/her name. The Cat's revenges are terrible and timeless.

'BOOKS IS COMIN',' yelled Mandy the Boot, blundering into the classroom in her father's size 12 army boots, and knocking Slasher Ormeroyd flying, which caused him to leap up with a mad roar and lurch to attack her, except that the Cat (Felix Delaney) paused in the middle of a poker game with Lia Tansy, Chinky Fred, and Tom Lightfinger to call out, 'Cool it, Slasher,' so that he hauled back his huge maulers for he always does what the Cat tells him. As we all do.

'What books?' enquired the Cat gently, for he was a great reader: crime and horror.

'A huge crate full. Old Perkins is turning 'em over an' oinkin' like a ma pig with piglets. There's hundreds.'

'Mr Pertins has comed back to us, doody, doody,' crooned Daisy Chain, blue eyes beaming, bright hair bobbing. She loved Mr Perkins, and he was fond of her, not that he had much choice, M 1 3 not being noted for its lovable characters. Mind you, we were all pleased to see him. He'd been absent on a course and the teacher they sent instead left in tears on Wednesday morning, making the rest of the week very tedious. The Headmaster took us. His name is Mr Bliss and it's a lie.

'That's great,' said Bat Pearson, resident genius. 'And about the books. We need new ones. Not that I read much fiction, haven't the time' – she was wading through *A Study of Bog Burial in Scandinavia and Europe* (funny place to bury people, said Mandy) – 'but I like to keep Killer going and he can't stand *Little Women*.'

Killer, six feet two and growing, nodded, for Bat does all his work. In return he's her Minder. Most of us need one. M I 3 aren't popular in the school, not that they're popular out of it either.

'I like Enid Blyton,' cried Hot Chocolate, the class prefect. 'I've read them all. Sir once said they'd made me what I am.'

'Belt up,' bellowed Hag Stevens from the doorway. 'Mr Perkins is on his way.' We were all so pleased to see him that we arranged ourselves nicely, looking keen and eager. And instead of sighing as he usually does at the sight of us, he smiled, which smoothed out all his wrinkles, like an American with a face lift.

'It's so nice to see you all again,' he said warmly, and as if that wasn't enough he was dressed in cords and check shirt. Where was his old chalky? What was up? 'As you know, I've been on a course, a language course, which I really enjoyed, and now I feel we can go forward with a new outlook.'

'A what . . .?' asked Brain Drain, dim even by M I 3's standards.

'A new outlook on the rest of our year together. Speaking to you honestly, as your friend as well as teacher, that course came just in the nick of time, for I'd begun to despair at the thought of us struggling and drowning together . . .'

'I wunt let yer drown, Sir,' interrupted Brain Drain, breathing hard, for uttering more than two words was always difficult. 'I kin swim.'

'Quite,' Sir agreed. 'Now let's see if my old friends are all here . . . Abdullah, Asra, Brian . . .'

Killer and Slasher were despatched to carry in the heavy crate, Bat, Lia and Mandy to organize the class resource centre. The rest of the school has a central area, but it was decided that M I 3 should just keep theirs in the classroom, after Tom Lightfinger flogged all the cassette players and musical instruments to some teenage pals to start a group.

'Any 'orror comics or girlie mags?' Slasher asked Killer hopefully.

'No, shurrup. The Cat looks after that side, and y'know he don't think it right for old Perkins to learn about such things. Not at his age.'

Eventually all the splendid new books were arranged and the classroom transformed. Mr Perkins had done well, something for everyone: *Dr Seuss* for Brain Drain and Daisy and the Heap, *War and Peace* for Bat, *An Anthology of Horror* for the Cat. He beamed at us all.

'Yes, you shall soon get at them, but first something new for a new day. Has anyone a poem for me? A suitable poem, mind, Ormeroyd.'

A mind-boggling hush fell for we always turned to the Cat or Bat or Mandy to represent us on these occasions and they all three despised poetry (wet, useless, boring). And then Brain Drain lumbered to his feet.

'I know one about an ickle worm.' And he recited it while Sir grinned like a maniac.

'Jolly good,' he cried. 'They told me it would work. Good old MI3. Don't let me down. Surely you must know a poem, Beatrice.'

Bat stood up, grimacing horribly, embarrassed. 'The only one I know is a dead boring one from Horace, about a smelly, skinny youth. Dates back to my classical hang-up last year. Sorry. Will that do?'

Sir nodded, and the Latin phrases hung in the classroom already quite well-known for its language. Killer smiled approvingly. His Bat was doing well even if no one could understand a word of it. And Tom Lightfinger got up, brick red. 'Know one about a dicky bird,' he said, head down. 'Learnt it in the Infants.' One by one MI3 made their offerings, the Cat last, with the lyrics of an obscure cult rock group.

A week later anyone walking into MI3's classroom, and most people preferred not to, would have had to weave their way through poems everywhere – on the walls, on the windows,

standing in displays, hanging on string, swinging in mobiles, for
M I 3 had taken to poetry, writing poems, reading poems, reciting
poems, illustrating poems. Mr Perkins had seen a miracle in his
lifetime and walked on air. The school grapevine had it that the
class had either gone barmy or had reformed at last. Actually, it
was, as usual, the Cat.

Shoulders hunched, black glasses, white face, he said, 'I want
old Perkins happy. De poetry mikes him happy. So we get with de
poetry. See?' We saw.

When it wasn't poetry, it was stories. M I 3 went book-mad,
reading all of the time all over the place, even walking round the
playground reading, with Killer and Slasher there to settle anyone
foolish enough to find it funny. Those who understood what those
squiggles on a page meant helped those who didn't.

So occupied were we, we didn't notice that the school's big
issue was now Conservation. A famous celebrity had addressed the
school on the subject and projects mushroomed everywhere. But
it wasn't until a very pretty lady came to tell the school of the
plight of a butterfly that was about to die out unless money could
be raised to provide a Nature Reserve where it could breed that
M I 3 realized it was needed.

'Dat poor ickle utterfly,' muttered Brain Drain, moved.

Now despite everything: lies, thefts, vandalism, dishonesty,
cheating, bullying, greed, truancy, you name it, M I 3's got it:
despite all these or as well as, M I 3 has Heart. Disasters, we weep
over disasters. Earthquakes bring contributions from us faster
than anyone. Tom Lightfinger has been known to pinch the Save
the Children pennies bottle from the corner shop to contribute to
the class's gift. So when the very pretty lady said there was to be a
prize for the best school contribution – a silver medal – and a
framed poem about a butterfly written by the very pretty lady
herself for the best class collection, there could be no doubt about
it. M I 3 intended to get that prize, that poem on their wall.

No one needed to tell M I 3 about fund-raising. We have a

natural talent for it: begging, gambling, sponsoring, busking, collecting, blackmailing, grovelling, stealing, shop-lifting, extorting, bullying, even selling, we went about it all in the way that suited each of us best. Yet in the final week but one, the grapevine informed the Cat that Hadley Grove School were the favourites, their rich parents being plushier than ours.

Mr Perkins was heard to remark with pleasure on the industry of his class, most pleased, most pleased. Reading, writing and money-raising thrived. An experienced teacher, though, every Friday he collected in the books that had worked the miracle (he thought) and checked them. That Friday only Bat's was missing and she promised faithfully etc. Mr Perkins went home. Happy.

On Monday morning all the shelves were empty. All the books had disappeared. So had every leaflet, magazine, poster and map in the resources area. His face sagged back into all those wrinkles, and he took the register, all present, except for Brain Drain.

'Right, what have you lot done with them?' He didn't look at all like that nice Mr Perkins. He looked more like Hanging Judge Jeffreys.

'Delaney, what have you organized?'

'Nothing, Sir.' The Cat at a loss, for once. 'Honest.'

'You don't know what honesty is, Delaney.'

But the Cat stood firm; it was nothing to do with him nor anyone else that he knew of.

'Then, Lightfinger, it just has to be you.'

'No, no, no. I liked the books. They just took what I was half-way in the middle of and I haven't finished. And I dint read the ending first, for once.'

'Hard luck,' snapped Mr Perkins, cruelly.

And the door crashed open as the vast, shaggy head of Brain Drain appeared first, then the rest of him, waving a fistful of money.

'For de utterfly pome, Mr Perkins. For de pome. We win it now, won't we? Look at all de lolly. And I did it for you, Mr Perkins, becos you give me all dem pomes and I love pomes now.'

'Brian, look at me and stop gabbling. Where did you get that money? And do you know what's happened to all our books?'

'I've conserved our books. Dey'll go on f'ever an' ever. An' dey gived me lolly for 'em. Look.'

'But how?' groaned Mr Perkins.

Brain Drain was panting like an old train at full steam ahead. 'Me auntie Mave. Cleanin' after school, an' she give me this dustbin bag an' I put 'em all in an' took 'em to our church for rebikin' . . .'

'For what?' Mr Perkins looked as if he was going demented.

'Recycling,' translated Bat.

'An' they said what a good cause, and gived me money an' we'll win the pome now, wun't we?' he beamed. He sat down and then bobbed up again in the heavy silence. 'Mr Perkins, Sir?'

'Yes, Brian?' came a low moan.

'I conserved them books and the utterfly, dint I?'

'Oh, Brian, you did, you did.'

After a long time the Cat spoke, and for possibly the first time in his life his voice was full of pity.

'M13. Listen. De kindness, get it? From now on we are going to be kind to Mr Perkins.'

How M13 visited the recycling plant, rescued all the books (not very suitable anyway, they said), was spotted by the Mayor, also visiting, got its picture in all the papers (such keen children), won the school medal and the butterfly poem (more pictures in the papers – what fine, hardworking children, an example to others), so that at last Brain Drain could hang the pome on the wall – except they'd gone on to computer games by then – and as usual were hated bitterly by the rest of the school (good, hardworking, boring children) is another story.

Bud's Luck

PETER DAVIDSON

BUD WAS FLITTING from one-arm bandit to one-arm bandit, feeling in the payout cups for odd coins. He'd already shaken 3 pence out of the Penny Falls machine and he needed to find 2 more pence to make 5 to change into a 5 pence piece and then . . . Then he could play his favourite pin-ball machine.

He had arrived in Funlandia, the arcade he always went to, at about 2 o'clock. He spent the morning wandering up and down Oxford Street, his eyes glued to the floor. Or he walked around the department stores searching for money that people had dropped. He remembered how he once found a pound. But today he had found a colourful collection of buttons and just enough money for six goes on the pin-ball machine. Mainly because that woman with the purple coat and the shopping basket had been following him around the shop. Bud was sure she was a store detective.

The thuck of the machine recording a free game woke Bud from his dream and he drifted over and watched the man play. He was good, better than Bud, and his mates thought Bud was an expert.

The man played his game and left. Bud dejectedly tapped the machine with his boot. Then, as his anger at not having enough money grew, he gave it a much heavier kick. The machine rattled and the lights went out. Bud heard a familiar sound. The clink of a reject coin. There in the cup was a 5 pence piece.

Bud nearly fell over himself as he dived to grab it. He crammed it into the slot and prepared himself to play. The game went well, and Bud was proud of his performance. The last ball disappeared and the game ended and Bud made to walk away, pleased at his good fortune.

Then he heard it – 'Clink!' The 5 pence was there in the cup again. 'Great,' thought Bud, and back it went into the machine. And again and again. Each time the coin came back.

Bud began to wonder if perhaps there was something wrong with the pintable. So he tried a different one. The same thing happened. Clink, back it came.

So he tried a different machine. Clink, and back it came. Bud began to think that there was something special about the 5 pence. He decided to risk losing it one more time in a one-arm bandit. His hands were sweating so much he drooped his 5 pence piece. But it didn't roll anywhere. It fell and stayed, just by his right foot. Bud bent down and picked it up and slowly, fearing that he would lose his lucky coin, he placed it in the slot of the one-arm bandit. He pulled the handle. The drums spun around, and one by one stopped. He lost. But there in the reject coin cup sat the 5 pence piece. Bud smiled, and the 5 pence seemed to smile back.

He carefully picked it up and clutching it in his hand walked out of Funlandia.

Bud couldn't remember how he got home. He thought he could remember getting in a one-man bus, putting his 5 pence piece into the ticket machine, getting his ticket and his money back. Did he get off a stop later than he should have done? His brain was running wild. He was thinking frantically of how he could make his magic 5 pence work for him to make him rich.

'I'm starving. What's for tea?' Bud's mum said these words, as he came in the back door.

'Well. I *am* starving and what *is* for tea?'

Bud didn't talk to his mum much and these were usually the only words he said between arriving home, eating whatever his mum had cooked up and going out again. He spent his evenings wandering the streets, or hanging around the garages at the back of the flats with his friends.

He raced through his beefburgers and chips, then went to watch a bit of telly. But his dad was sprawled in the arm chair, snoring. Snoring loud enough to drown the sound.

Bud screwed his hand into the pocket of his jeans, made sure the 5 pence was there, got up, zipped on his jacket and slipped out of the door.

Bud didn't go directly to the garages. He walked and ran to the local papershop. Outside it on the wall were a chewing-gum machine and a chocolate machine and just in the doorway was a machine that sold bubbly-gum and plastic balls with rubber frogs and spiders inside.

It took him about 4 minutes to empty the machines. The magic 5 pence was working well. It went through the machines as smoothly as Guinness went through his dad.

Bud pocketed the 5 pence. He tucked his jumper in his jeans, poured the packets of chewing-gum and the plastic bubbles and the chocolate down the Vee-neck till they made a comforting bulge on his stomach, then zipped up his jacket and strolled off to the garages.

'Hello. Here comes Flowerbud,' shouted Billy.

'Hi Billy, Eric,' returned Bud.

As he walked towards them he remembered how he came to be called Bud. His real name was Timothy Flower, and one day, someone had called him 'Flowerbud'. Somehow the Bud bit had stuck with him. He didn't mind – he liked being called Bud.

'What have you got up your jacket?' Billy was the first to speak.

'Nothing much.' Bud hadn't yet decided if he was going to tell his friends about the magic 5 pence or not.

'Come on, show us.' This time it was Eric and he was already pulling at Bud's jacket, eager to see what was hidden. Billy quickly joined in the pulling and tugging of Bud's jacket, and Bud tried hard to fight them off. But their scrabbling hands were impossible to hold off. Out it all tumbled. The chewing-gum, the plastic bubbles and the chocolate. They formed a little pile at the boys' feet, the silver paper of the chocolate bars glinting temptingly in the dull light from the curtained windows.

There was a pause of a heart-beat.

Then down! All three boys fell to their knees with their hands scooping up the chocolate bars, the plastic bubbles, the chewing-gum.

'Where did you get this lot?' gasped Billy.

Then came the lie. Bud had made his decision. He would keep his 5 pence a secret.

'I smashed open a few machines.'

'Where?'

'Go on, tell us.'

Bud answered slowly, as though he was really trying to hide something – which he was.

'Oh, you know – down-town.'

Billy and Eric could tell Bud was giving nothing away, so they stopped asking him. A long silence followed, while each of the boys thought things over. Then Bud spoke.

'Well, give me back my stuff then.'

The two boys looked at him, looked at each other, and then said together, 'Your stuff!'

'Well it is mine.'

Eric answered.

'*Was*. It's shared three ways now, and that's how it will stay.'

Bud was now beginning to believe his lie himself. The two friends squared up to Bud and said, coldly, almost spitting in his face, 'Either share or you get none.'

Bud didn't know what to do, so in his confusion he threw down his sweets and with a 'Well if that's how you want it' turned his back on his friends and walked off into the night.

Billy and Eric watched him go, and they noticed that his right hand suddenly shot into his pocket, and as it did his shoulders seemed to pull back, and his head, instead of being aimed at the ground, seemed to look up dreamily at the black sky.

'You're nuts,' yelled Eric at his disappearing back.

Bud's plan was slowly forming in his mind. What happened tonight with Billy and Eric was never going to happen again. He didn't care if he never spoke to them again. His right fist clenched around his 5 pence as he thought that with that he didn't need friends.

He was going to empty every machine in the district and every machine that he could get to by one-man operated bus. He would make his 5 pence work for him. He would sell what he got from the machines at half price and be a millionaire by the time he was twenty-one.

Bud went home by way of a few other machines he knew. Supplies for his first day's trading were well tucked under his jacket, as he shouted 'Goodnight' to his mum and dad and ran upstairs to bed.

It was break the next day. Word had quickly got round school that Bud was selling stuff worth 5 pence for 2 pence.

'Got any chocolate left?'

'Yeah, two bars.'

'I'll have them.'

'OK.'

Trade was brisk. By the end of break everything was gone.

No-one even bothered to ask where Bud got the sweets from. No-one bothered to ask, but Billy and Eric were watching, and they just couldn't figure out where Bud was getting the stuff. They didn't think that he had it in him to smash machines. They almost knew that they were right.

That night on the way home, Bud bought a haversack from the Army and Navy stores, to collect his sweets in. He spent the night riding around on buses and filling his haversack.

He put the bag under his bed. He put the magic 5 pence inside his sock and inside his boot. He slid himself into bed and dreamed of his first Rolls Royce.

The next day at school, Bud sold his sweets and chewing-gum, through break and right through dinner time. He thought that everything was going just fine. He reckoned without Billy and Eric. They tried to apologise for what had happened two nights ago, but Bud wouldn't listen.

They knew what they were going to do. They would follow him from machine to machine, off bus and onto bus, and it cost them a good deal of money to do it.

The first Bud knew of their following him was the rush of feet through leaves as they ran up to him from behind. He turned to face them.

'Right, hand it over.' Eric was first to speak.

'What?' was all Bud could manage to say.

'You know,' hissed Billy.

Bud held out the haversack and Eric just kicked it out of his hand, into the gutter.

'Not that – the coin. The one that you use on the machines.'

'I haven't got one.'

It was a daft thing to say. It was the last straw. Billy and Eric had just had enough of him.

They jumped on him, and started punching, kneeing, kicking all over Bud's body. He tried to fight them off, but it was hopeless. After a long fight and with Bud's nose streaming blood, Eric held Bud's arms while Billy felt through his pockets.

He soon found what he was looking for, and with a triumphant yell he held the 5 pence up for Eric to see. The two boys whooped with delight. They let Bud fall to the floor and walked off, flicking the coin between themselves.

Bud waited until they had gone, picked up his sack, and dragged himself home. He was angry at the loss of his 5 pence. Angry at Billy and Eric for beating him up. Angry at himself for being stupid enough to let himself be followed. Most of all his right fist felt empty without the 5 pence.

He didn't bother to say 'Goodnight' when he got home. He just went to bed.

As Bud was putting his sock on in the morning, he felt something cold between his toes. He ripped his sock off. The 5 pence fell to the floor and didn't roll – just stayed by his right foot. Bud was glad to have his coin back. Puzzled, but glad.

When he got to school, with his haversack of course – business must go on – he met Billy and Eric. They both had long faces.

'We lost the bloody thing in a machine and got no chocolate.'

'Oh,' said Bud and smiled. Well done, 5 pence!

The smile was soon to be knocked from his face. Billy and Eric spread the word about the magic 5 pence and every night a gang of boys followed him home, beat him up and took the coin. And every morning it was there in his sock.

He was still selling sweets, but he was beginning to wonder if the beatings up were worth the hundreds of 2 pences he had collected.

He began to fear all the boys in his school. He had no friends. Each time he was beaten up and somebody else used his coin, the machine would keep the coin, and not give anything out. No gum, no chocolate, no nothing.

Bud's old friends now hated him.

Bud now hated the coin, but he didn't want to throw it away. What about his Rolls Royce?

Time went on, and word spread to neighbouring schools. Bud had taken to leaving the coin at home, so that when boys came to fight him for it he could tell them he hadn't got it.

They never listened. They always beat him up. Held his arms, and there in his pocket found the 5 pence.

And every morning it was back in his sock.

He tried to throw it away but each time he tried, his fingers just wouldn't let go. It always ended up in his pocket.

Then he got his idea.

He didn't go to school that day. He took an empty jam jar and a spoon from home. He took all the 2 pence pieces he had collected.

He bought a huge pack of polyfilla. Bud found a gents' toilet. Inside he mixed the polyfilla in the jam jar with some water until it made a thick paste. He then pushed the coin into the polyfilla and pressed it down with the spoon until it glinted at him through the bottom.

After what seemed hours of walking around, it had set.

Bud looked around for the bus stop he wanted and got on the bus when it came. He paid his fare with real money. The juddering of the bus disguised Bud's nervousness. The bus finally stopped where Bud wanted to be, and he got off.

The wind whipped his hair into his eyes, as he threw all the money he had made and the jam jar full of polyfilla and the 5 pence piece over the side of Waterloo Bridge into the dark waters of the river.

The blood was pounding so hard in his head that Bud didn't even hear the splash.

He turned away, put his hand in his pockets, and felt it there.

The Co'vit

ROBERT LEESON

I WAS IN my last year at our school when I had a row with my mates.

We fell out one Saturday over where we wanted to go. I wanted to go to Millbury Woods. Harold and Jammy wanted to go to the Hall.

'You can't get up to the Hall, any road,' I said grumpily. 'The gamekeepers'll stop you. Tommy Mills got shot up there.'

'That's what he says. He's a rotten ligger,' said Harold.

'Hey,' said Jammy. 'Come on. It's smashing up at the Hall once you get in over the wall.'

'Yeah, I know,' I jeered, 'miles and miles of wet rhodondendrons.' But I spoiled the sneer because I couldn't say the word let alone spell it.

'Nah,' Jammy grinned. 'I heard Dad say there's a lot of statues there, women with nothing on and that. You don't find that in Millbury Woods.'

'There's better,' I said.

'Well, what?'

'Well, lots. There's the bridge, and the stream and boat racing.'

'Ah, that's ancient . . .'

I wanted to say – there's the co'vit. But I couldn't make myself utter the word. If I told the real truth I really didn't want them with me. Yet at the same time, I was a bit scared of being on my own.

So when Harold and Jammy said they wouldn't go to the woods, I was half pleased and half annoyed. I looked at Bella hoping she'd decide to come with me. But she didn't. She didn't even say:

'Aw, come on with us.'

In which case I might have changed my mind.

But she said nothing.

'All right,' said Harold, 'be on your own, you misery,' and they turned their backs and walked off up the road.

So in the end I set off for the woods in a bad mood. I was annoyed with them. And I was a bit annoyed with myself. The weather was hot and close. There hadn't been any rain for a fortnight and the fields were yellowing in the sun. The turf on top of Rabbit Hollow was brown, and heat haze was rising on the skyline. My wellies were tight on my feet and the sweat ran down my neck. By the time I got into the woods I had a headache and I was parched. I lay down on the bank above the bridge and had a drink from the stream. It tasted bitter and strange.

Under the trees the air was still and stuffy. Every move in the grass and bushes brought up a cloud of insects that settled on my face. Time and again as I trudged on upstream I wiped them off or flapped my hands to get rid of midges and gnats which hung in clouds over the water. The going became rougher as the ground sloped upwards. I noticed too that the woods were darker than usual. The sky, when I caught a glimpse of it through the trees, was a strange, darkish, steely colour, as though a big lid had been pulled across, and the woods, with me inside, were shut under it. There was no sound, no birds, no small animals rushing off in the bushes.

It was strange. It was as if the woods and the sky were waiting for something and I began to turn round to see if I were really alone.

Now I was in the high part of the woods, scrambling on the slippery overhang with the stream in its narrow bed beneath. The light grew dimmer, the great bank of the canal loomed up in front and the sky overhead had changed from steel grey to steel blue. The sun had vanished. I stopped to get my breath, hooking my arm over an overhanging branch. The culvert I knew was just ahead beyond a fold in the ground.

With a deep breath and a count of twenty I let go of my branch and half ran, half slipped over the rise in front of me and came right up against the huge wall of earth and grass that towered up above, holding the canal. Twenty yards to my right was the culvert, a black oval in the green. I sat down and slithered sideways over the sloping turf until I could steady myself on the moss-covered brick arch of the tunnel entrance.

A breath of damp, stagnant air came up and I shivered. Below me the stream coursed out of the ground, its waters foaming and gurgling over the brickwork. I could not tell how deep it was here. There was nothing for it but to go down. Digging my fingers into the brickwork set in the bank I lowered myself carefully down the six-foot drop to the bottom curve of the tunnel. Just as I tried to shift my hold to a crack in the lower brickwork, my foot slipped. Down I went, jarring shoulders and hip, landing on all fours in the water. I felt it flood into my wellies as I grabbed for the tunnel edge and hauled myself on to the brick curve above water level. The sides were green with slime and hard to hold on to. Three times I slid back before I got a proper grip and stood, clinging to the inner wall.

Ahead of me the tunnel stretched dark and cold, but at the end was a faint oval of light, like the far mouth of the canal at Tunnel Top.

But this was larger and nearer. I reckoned it was fifty yards to the other side. I put a foot out along the brickwork, slipped and found myself sliding into the water again, but clutched in time at a split in the brickwork. My hands were coated with slime now, but I held on. I had no choice. I could not move forward without slipping. Nor could I move back without letting go. Behind, the woods were in thick gloom; ahead, the tunnel even darker.

As I hung there, the sky over the bank split in a silver vein of forked lightning and a massive thunder clap shook the bank. I thought my eardrums would meet in the middle of my head. Without thinking I clapped hands to my ears, let go of the brickwork and went sliding down the greasy circle of the wall into the water. At the last moment I saved myself by throwing my body across the channel so that my hands struck flat against the opposite wall. I was clear of the water but stretched out across it like a mad diver, not falling down but not able to get upright again.

Outside, more lightning. The thunder rang down the tunnel till I thought the whole bank, canal and all, would give way and bury me. I remembered all Ollie had said about the land caving in and my inside went cold. I tried to push up with my hands but the strength was gone from my arms. Yet I couldn't stay there. I knew that. I told myself, saying it out loud. But I could not push upright. Arms and legs were numb with strain, stomach chilled with fright.

The rain was flooding down outside now and as I looked at the stream rushing down the channel below me, I noticed something that made my heart give a jump. The water was turning brown. I knew right away what that meant. The water beyond the canal was rising, the mud stirred up in the stream bed. Before long it would come through the narrow hole in a torrent.

The thought gave me strength. I jerked both hands from the wall and tried to come upright again. But fell back. This time, though, my hands had shifted a foot along the brickwork. To keep my body straight, I edged my feet sideways, farther into the tunnel.

It struck me right away. This was the way to go. Sideways. I jerked up my hands again and half-fell to the right, breaking my fall again, hands on wall. Then I shifted my feet again and again. I was moving like a crab about a yard a minute, but I was moving. Forgetting the thunder, the lightning, the flood water, my fears, everything, I set my mind on getting through that tunnel. At the end of the culvert the white circle grew lighter and lighter. I made out the stream on the other side, high green banks and overhanging willow trees. Beyond that a slope with more trees. I speeded up, slipping and sliding now and then, but more sure of my feet and hands, until with three last sideways heaves I was on a ledge at the lip of the tunnel on the other side. I was through and at the edge of the little green valley with the stream now foaming with flood water in front of me.

Overhead the thunder died away, the rain stopped and above the trees the dark sky opened into blue, grey and white streaks. As I jumped from the ledge to the bank of the stream to clamber to the top, the sun came through, suddenly warm on the back of my neck. At the top of the valley I paused and looked back. Behind me the great canal embankment and the tree tops beyond. But ahead!

I stood and stared. From my vantage point I could see a whole new world, great patches of water glinting in the sun, islands with purple flowering bushes, huge weed-covered cinder heaps, ravines filled with shrubs, a winding track and broken white bridge, and beyond, roofs and walls half sunk into the water. I felt like every explorer since time began. With a yell I rushed down the track towards the bridge. Halfway there I stopped and turned aside to peer down into a gully, full from top to bottom with blackberry bushes, a mass of blossom. Wait till I told our Mam. We'd pick tons of berries here in August and September.

Running on I caught with the corner of my eye the shine of sun on glass. To my left was a ruined house, like a farm.

Leading up to it was a splendid row of white-and-pink-blossomed horse chestnut trees. There'd be millions of conkers in a few months' time.

I followed the track where it ran, banked up with ash and cinders between the flashes. Now it wound up to a ridge and as I mounted this I saw I was only on the edge of my discovery. Before me was a great stretch of bush-studded moor, with larger lakes, clumps of small trees and like an ancient city, the ruins of old workings, a network of grass- and moss-covered walls forming caverns and arches, trenches and dugouts. I dodged madly among the ruins, peering here, poking there, noting in my mind places to explore when I had more time.

Beyond the workings, more open space with more blackberry bushes than I'd ever seen in my life. Farther off still, more flashes glinting in the hot sun. At first I did not grasp it, but these flashes did not reflect the sky. They had their own colour, a weird emerald green and whitey blue. It was not water, but a great expanse of chemical waste stretching in front of me, dead like some landscape on the Moon. I pulled a brick from a broken wall and hurled it into the nearest pool. It rested a second on the green crust and then sank slowly into the ooze.

I looked round me now, for I'd been running and charging round for about an hour. The woods and canal were well behind me. I was alone in my own fantastic world. But where was I?

Then I saw on the skyline, the unmistakable great grey-brown plume of smoke that marked the Works. I headed towards it and beyond the last green-blue lake, came to a final ridge and looked down into the valley, at the curve of the river and farther along the wooded hill that marked home. Half an hour later I'd reached the canal a mile or so from Tarcroft and was trotting along the tow path. I ran easily as if my excitement had given me a second wind. The damp in my clothes had dried in the sun. As I ran, the Works buzzer sounded across the river.

I stopped, alarmed. Was that the twelve o'clock or the one o'clock?

Down the slope I saw the men on foot and on bike, stream over the bridge. They were heading away from the Works. It was twelve o'clock. It was amazing. All the things I'd done and I'd only been away three hours and I could get home easily for dinner. It was just right, smashing, a bonzer day and all on my own.

After dinner I rushed out in the street. I wasn't going to call for Jammy or Harold or Bella, oh no. But if they happened to be around . . . I might just tell them a bit of what they'd missed. But there was no sign of them. They must have gone off somewhere. I felt flat after the morning's excitement.

I trailed off along the Lane, half hoping they might be there, but the Lane was empty. I wandered round corners and side turnings until I heard shouting in the distance. There was a football game on the rec. Might as well go and watch. It wasn't a real game, just a crowd of kids booting a ball between the goal posts, charging about in a big crowd, changing position. Even the goalie was up with the rest, trying to score.

The ball shot out of the scrimmage and landed near my feet. I belted it back and a lad trapped it with his foot. He grinned and waved. It was Tosher.

'Hey up. Come on. You can be on our side.'

I didn't waste any more time but rushed in kicking with the rest. 'Haven't seen you down here in donkey's years,' said Tosher.

'Been doing things. Hey up, Tosher, there's a smashing place down the canal . . .'

Anti-snore Machine

ROBIN KLEIN

MARTINE KIRBY WAS good-natured and generous. Also, her father owned a chocolate factory, so when it was time for the school camp, everyone wanted to be in her room. In fact so many people wanted to that Miss Lewis, the teacher in charge of the camp, finally had to draw lots. Tracey, Paula and Bronwyn won. Tracey and Paula were extremely pleased, but not about having to share with Bronwyn, who was Tracey's little sister.

Everyone had terrific fun that first night, doing all the usual things such as filling each other's shower caps with talcum powder, and fighting over who was going to have the only top bunk. 'I don't mind not having it,' Martine said generously. 'I sleep like a log, anyhow, no matter where I am.'

So Paula and Tracey felt ashamed of being greedy, and let her have the top bunk. (Also, they remembered about the midnight feast and her Dad owning a chocolate factory.)

'Showers, PJs and lights out at ten,' Miss Lewis said. 'Anyone talking after that will have to sleep in the creek with the bunyips.'

But the midnight feast went on much longer. Martine shared all the sweets her Dad had given her with everyone along the corridor. All that glucose gave everyone a tremendous surge of renewed energy, and Miss Lewis stopped calling out indulgently, 'Girls, put the lights out now, please,' She yelled instead, 'LIGHTS OUT THIS MINUTE STOP THAT TALKING AND I WON'T SAY IT ONE MORE TIME!' So everyone knew she meant it and shovelled the chocolate wrappers off their beds and got ready to go to sleep.

Martine Kirby didn't have any trouble at all. She blinked once or twice at the ceiling, shut her eyes and fell asleep instantly.

And snored.

It wasn't ordinary snoring. It could best be described as a combination of a hippopotamus with sinus trouble, an electric sander, a truck dumping a load of gravel, peak-hour traffic along a six-lane motorway and a dam bursting its banks.

Everyone sat up in bed saying polite things such as, 'I say, Martine, do you mind . . .' and 'Martine, excuse me, but do you realize . . .' But none of that had any effect and they started to bellow at her instead. They all had their hands clapped over their ears to block out the sound of Martine snoring, and didn't realize how loudly they were yelling until Miss Lewis opened the door, glaring.

She wasn't very sympathetic. 'You'll just have to get used to it,' she said crossly. 'One person snoring shouldn't keep everyone else awake. Put some cotton wool in your ears.'

So they tried cotton wool, plus shredded tissues and the hoods of their sleeping bags over that, but nothing could blot out the sound of Martine Kirby's snoring. She kept it up all night, not missing one single beat. In the morning she bounced out of bed, glowing with health and rest, all ready for a brisk five-kilometre run before breakfast. No one else in that room looked rested. They all had tired red eyes and weary expressions.

'We couldn't get any sleep all night because of your snoring!' Tracey and Paula said.

'I didn't know I was snoring,' Martine said apologetically. 'I always sleep so soundly. Though come to think of it, maybe that's the reason why my sister Angela moved out of our room and into the garage. But I'll try not to snore tonight. I promise.'

Promises are all very well.

That next night, Martine put on an astonishing performance, as though the previous night's snoring had just been a practice run. You might as well have tried to get to sleep in a cathedral belfry with all the bell-ringers and their understudies practising Christmas carols.

'We can't go a whole week without sleep,' Tracey said desperately.

'We could try —' Bronwyn said shyly, but she was frowned at for daring to speak.

'I'll just have to invent a special machine that cures snoring,' said Paula, who came from a long line of engineers. Seeing that it was useless to think about sleep while Martine was not only thinking about it but doing it successfully enough for a whole army, Tracey sat on Paula's bed and watched her design a snoring machine on a sheet of paper.

'It looks very complicated,' Tracey said doubtfully. 'And it's going to be hard to get all those things in the middle of the night.'

'Why couldn't we —' said Bronwyn, but Paula and Tracey hit her with a pillow and told her to mind her own business.

'This is how my machine works,' said Paula. 'I'll stickytape a paper bag, open end down, on the wall just above Martine's face. Above the bag there'll be a sheet of cardboard. Fixed to that will be a glove stuffed with something heavy, like a boxing glove. Above the glove will be another board, and poised on one end will be a heavy object, such as a desert boot. Just below the desert boot, on Martine's bedside table, there's a ruler balanced over a matchbox, and on the other end of the ruler, there's a bowl of water. And in the bowl of water the thickest, soggiest sponge we can find.'

'Much easier to —' said Bronwyn, but Paula and Tracey turned round and looked at her as though she were some kind of worm.

'Martine's snoring will inflate the paper bag,' said Paula. 'The bag of breath will push against the cardboard. The cardboard will push up the glove which will punch the board holding the heavy object. The heavy object will fall on to the ruler edge which will tip the saucer of water and the sponge right in to the middle of Martine Kirby's snoring and make her shut up!'

'Wow!' said Tracey, but Bronwyn didn't say anything. She just looked as though she didn't think that that machine would work. But Paula and Tracey made her go out into the dark corridor and into the craft room and search around till she found all the things necessary for Paula's invention. It would have been hard to find her way back to their room in the dark, but Martine's snoring served as a very good beacon.

Paula built the machine, and when it was finished, she and Tracey looked at it with admiration. Paula even took a flashlight picture of it for her files.

'I don't think it will work,' Bronwyn said, but no one took any notice of her at all.

It was as though Martine knew, even in her sleep, that some momentous experiment was taking place, for her snoring grew even louder than the previous night. Very slowly the paper bag above her face began to swell. It billowed like a balloon and pushed against the cardboard shelf. The glove, stuffed with chocolate papers and socks, moved too. It rapped the board above, and the carefully balanced desert boot slipped off, as clean as an anchor. The desert boot crashed down on the ruler edge. The saucer of water and the sponge jumped into the air and landed with a loud wet splosh right in Martine Kirby's face.

'zzzzzzzzzzz zzzzzzzzzzzzz,' she said, without even flickering an eyelash.

Paula burst into tears of disappointment, thwarted genius and sheer exhaustion from having no sleep for two nights running. Tracey tried to comfort her, but it's hard to murmur soothing words against a background of trumpeting snores.

'I'll ring up my Mum and get her to come and pick me up,' Paula said, sniffing. 'I'm not going to miss a whole week's sleep.'

'Me neither,' said Tracey. 'Is there room for my things in your Mum's car?'

'I don't want to go home yet and miss camp,' Bronwyn said. 'Anyhow, I think I can —'

'WHO TOLD YOU YOU COULD JOIN IN GROWN-UP CONVERSATION!' Tracey and Paula both said indignantly.

' – stop Martine's snoring,' Bronwyn finished. She stood on her bed and very gently turned Martine Kirby off her back and on to her side.

'There,' Bronwyn said into the sudden calm of the snoreless room. 'That's how you stop people snoring.'

Nothing to be Afraid of

JAN MARK

'ROBIN WON'T GIVE give you any trouble,' said Auntie Lynn. 'He's very quiet.'

Anthea knew how quiet Robin was. At present he was sitting under the table and, until Auntie Lynn mentioned his name, she had forgotten that he was there.

Auntie Lynn put a carrier bag on the armchair.

'There's plenty of clothes, so you won't need to do any washing, and there's a spare pair of pyjamas in case – well, you know. In case . . .'

'Yes,' said Mum, firmly. 'He'll be all right. I'll ring you tonight and let you know how he's getting along.' She looked at the clock. 'Now, hadn't *you* better be getting along?'

She saw Auntie Lynn to the front door and Anthea heard them saying good-bye to each other. Mum almost told Auntie Lynn to stop worrying and have a good time, which would have been a mistake because Auntie Lynn was going up North to a funeral.

Auntie Lynn was not really an Aunt, but she had once been at school with Anthea's mum, and she was the kind of person who couldn't manage without a handle to her name; so Robin was not Anthea's cousin. Robin was not anything much, except four years old, and he looked a lot younger; probably because nothing ever happened to him. Auntie Lynn kept no pets that might give Robin germs, and never bought him toys that had sharp corners to dent him or wheels that could be swallowed. He wore balaclava helmets and bobble hats in winter to protect his tender ears, and a knitted vest under his shirt in summer in case he overheated himself and caught a chill from his own sweat.

'Perspiration,' said Auntie Lynn.

His face was as pale and flat as a saucer of milk, and his eyes floated in it like drops of cod-liver oil. This was not so surprising as he was full to the back teeth with cod-liver oil; also with extract of malt, concentrated orange juice and calves-foot jelly. When you picked him up you expected him to squelch, like a hot-water bottle full of half-set custard.

Anthea lifted the tablecloth and looked at him.

'Hello, Robin.'

Robin stared at her with his flat eyes and went back to sucking his woolly doggy that had flat eyes also, of sewn-on felt, because glass ones might find their way into Robin's appendix and cause damage. Anthea wondered how long it would be before he noticed that his mother had gone. Probably he wouldn't, any more than he would notice when she came back.

Mum closed the front door and joined Anthea in looking under the table at Robin. Robin's mouth turned down at the corners, and Anthea hoped he would cry so that they could cuddle him. It seemed impolite to cuddle him before he needed it. Anthea was afraid to go any closer.

'What a little troll,' said Mum, sadly, lowering the tablecloth. 'I suppose he'll come out when he's hungry.'

Anthea doubted it.

Robin didn't want any lunch or any tea.

'Do you think he's pining?' said Mum. Anthea did not. Anthea had a nasty suspicion that he was like this all the time. He went to bed without making a fuss and fell asleep before the light was out, as if he were too bored to stay awake. Anthea left her bedroom door open, hoping that he would have a nightmare so that she could go in and comfort him, but Robin slept all night without a squeak, and woke in the morning as flat-faced as before. Wall-eyed Doggy looked more excitable than Robin did.

'If only we had a proper garden,' said Mum, as Robin went under the table again, leaving his breakfast eggs scattered round the plate. 'He might run about.'

Anthea thought that this was unlikely, and in any case they didn't have a proper garden, only a yard at the back and a stony strip in front, without a fence.

'Can I take him to the park?' said Anthea.

Mum looked doubtful. 'Do you think he wants to go?'

'No,' said Anthea, peering under the tablecloth. 'I don't think he wants to do anything, but he can't sit there all day.'

'I bet he can,' said Mum. 'Still, I don't think he should. All right, take him to the park, but keep quiet about it. I don't suppose Lynn thinks you're safe in traffic.'

'He might tell her.'

'Can he talk?'

Robin, still clutching wall-eyed Doggy, plodded beside her all the way to the park, without once trying to jam his head between the library railings or get run over by a bus.

'Hold my hand, Robin,' Anthea said as they left the house, and he clung to her like a lamprey.

The park was not really a park at all; it was a garden. It did not even pretend to be a park and the notice by the gate said KING STREET GARDENS, in case anyone tried to use it as a park. The grass was as green and as flat as the front-room carpet, but the front-room carpet had a path worn across it from the door to the fireplace, and here there were more notices that said KEEP OFF THE GRASS, so that the gritty white paths went obediently round the edge, under the orderly trees that stood in a row like the queue outside a fish shop. There were bushes in each corner and one shelter with a bench in it. Here and there brown holes in the grass, full of raked earth, waited for next year's flowers, but there were no flowers now, and the bench had been taken out of the shelter because the shelter was supposed to be a summer-house, and you couldn't have people using a summer-house in winter.

Robin stood by the gates and gaped, with Doggy depending limply from his mouth where he held it by one ear, between his teeth. Anthea decided that if they met anyone she knew, she would explain that Robin was only two, but very big for his age.

'Do you want to run, Robin?'

Robin shook his head.

'There's nothing to be afraid of. You can go all the way round, if you like, but you mustn't walk on the grass or pick things.'

Robin nodded. It was the kind of place that he understood. Anthea sighed. 'Well, let's walk round, then.'

They set off. At each corner, where the bushes were, the path diverged. One part went in front of the bushes, one part round the back of them. On the first circuit Robin stumped glumly beside Anthea in front of the bushes. The second time round she felt a very faint tug at her hand. Robin wanted to go his own way.

This called for a celebration. Robin could think. Anthea crouched down on the path until they were at the same level.

'You want to walk round the back of the bushes, Robin?'

'Yiss,' said Robin.

Robin could *talk*.

'All right, but listen.' She lowered her voice to a whisper. 'You must be very careful. That path is called Leopard Walk. Do you know what a leopard is?'

'Yiss.'

'There are two leopards down there. They live in the bushes. One is a good leopard and the other's a bad leopard. The good leopard has black spots. The bad leopard has red spots. If you see the bad leopard you must say, 'Die leopard die or I'll kick you in the eye,' and run like anything. Do you understand?'

Robin tugged again.

'Oh no,' said Anthea. 'I'm going *this* way. If you want to go down Leopard Walk, you'll have to go on your own. I'll meet you at the other end. Remember, if it's got red spots, run like mad.'

Robin trotted away. The bushes were just high enough to hide him, but Anthea could see the bobble on his hat doddering along. Suddenly the bobble gathered speed and Anthea had to run to reach the end of the bushes first.

'Did you see the bad leopard?'

'No,' said Robin, but he didn't look too sure.

'Why were you running then?'

'I just wanted to.'

'You've dropped Doggy,' said Anthea. Doggy lay on the path with his legs in the air, halfway down Leopard Walk.

'You get him,' said Robin.

'No, *you* get him,' said Anthea. 'I'll wait here.' Robin moved off, reluctantly. She waited until he had recovered Doggy and then shouted, 'I can see the bad leopard in the bushes!' Robin raced back to safety. 'Did you say, "Die leopard die or I'll kick you in the eye"?' Anthea demanded.

'No,' Robin said, guiltily.

'Then he'll *kill* us,' said Anthea. 'Come on, run. We've got to get to that tree. He can't hurt us once we're under that tree.'

They stopped running under the twisted boughs of a weeping ash. 'This is a python tree,' said Anthea. 'Look, you can see the python wound round the trunk.'

'What's a python?' said Robin, backing off.

'Oh, it's just a great big snake that squeezes people to death,' said Anthea. 'A python could easily eat a leopard. That's why leopards won't walk under this tree, you see, Robin.'

Robin looked up. 'Could it eat us?'

'Yes, but it won't if we walk on our heels.' They walked on their heels to the next corner.

'Are there leopards down there?'

'No, but we must never go down there anyway. That's Poison Alley. All the trees are poisonous. They drip poison. If one bit of poison fell on your head, you'd die.'

'I've got my hat on,' said Robin, touching the bobble to make sure.

'It would burn right through your hat,' Anthea assured him. 'Right into your brains. *Fzzzzzzz.*'

They by-passed Poison Alley and walked on over the manhole cover that clanked.

'What's that?'

'That's the Fever Pit. If anyone lifts that manhole cover, they get a terrible disease. There's this terrible disease down there, Robin, and if the lid comes off, the disease will get out and people will die. I should think there's enough disease down there to kill everybody in this town. It's ever so loose, look.'

'Don't lift it! Don't lift it!' Robin screamed, and ran to the shelter for safety.

'Don't go in there,' yelled Anthea. 'That's where the Greasy Witch lives.' Robin bounced out of the shelter as though he were on elastic.

'Where's the Greasy Witch?'

'Oh, you can't see her,' said Anthea, 'but you can tell where she is because she smells so horrible. I think she must be somewhere about. Can't you smell her now?'

Robin sniffed the air and clasped Doggy more tightly.

'And she leaves oily marks wherever she goes. Look, you can see them on the wall.'

Robin looked at the wall. Someone had been very busy, if not the Greasy Witch. Anthea was glad on the whole that Robin could not read.

'The smell's getting worse, isn't it, Robin? I think we'd better go down here and then she won't find us.'

'She'll see us.'

'No, she won't. She can't see with her eyes because they're full of grease. She sees with her ears, but I expect they're all waxy. She's a filthy old witch, really.'

They slipped down a secret-looking path that went round the back of the shelter.

'Is the Greasy Witch down here?' said Robin, fearfully.

'I don't know,' said Anthea. 'Let's investigate.' They tiptoed round the side of the shelter. The path was damp and slippery. 'Filthy old witch. She's certainly *been* here,' said Anthea. 'I think she's gone now. I'll just have a look.'

She craned her neck round the corner of the shelter. There was a sort of glade in the bushes, and in the middle was a stand-pipe, with a tap on top. The pipe was lagged with canvas, like a scaly skin.

'Frightful Corner,' said Anthea. Robin put his cautious head round the edge of the shelter.

'What's that?'

Anthea wondered if it could be a dragon, up on the tip of its tail and ready to strike, but on the other side of the bushes was the brick back wall of the King Street Public Conveniences, and at that moment she heard the unmistakable sound of a cistern flushing.

'It's a Lavatory Demon,' she said. 'Quick! We've got to get away before the water stops, or he'll have us.'

They ran all the way to the gates, where they could see the church clock, and it was almost time for lunch.

Auntie Lynn fetched Robin home next morning, and three days later she was back again, striding up the path like a warrior queen going into battle, with Robin dangling from her hand, and Doggy dangling from Robin's hand.

Mum took her into the front room, closing the door. Anthea sat on the stairs and listened. Auntie Lynn was in full throat and furious, so it was easy enough to hear what she had to say.

'I want a word with that young lady,' said Auntie Lynn. 'And I want to know what she's been telling him.' Her voice dropped, and Anthea could hear only certain fateful words: 'Leopards . . . poison trees . . . snakes . . . diseases!'

Mum said something very quietly that Anthea did not hear, and then Auntie Lynn turned up the volume once more.

'Won't go to bed unless I leave the door open . . . wants the light on . . . up and down to him all night . . . won't go to the bathroom on his own. He says the – the – ,' she hesitated, 'the *toilet* demons will get him. He nearly broke his neck running downstairs this morning.'

Mum spoke again, but Auntie Lynn cut in like a band-saw.

'Frightened out of his wits! He follows me everywhere.'

The door opened slightly, and Anthea got ready to bolt, but it was Robin who came out, with his thumb in his mouth and circles round his eyes. Under his arm was soggy Doggy, ears chewed to nervous rags.

Robin looked up at Anthea through the bannisters.

'Let's go to the park,' he said.

The Poison Ladies

H. E. BATES

WHEN YOU ARE only four, seven is a hundred and five inches are a mile.

Ben was seven and I was four and there were five inches between us. Ben also had big brown leather patches on the seat of his moley corduroy trousers and dark hairs on his legs and a horn-handled knife with two blades, a corkscrew and a thing he called a stabber.

'Arter we git through the fence,' Ben said, 'we skive round the sloe bushes and under them ash trees and then we're in the lane and arter that there's millions and millions o' poison berries. Don't you eat no poison berries, will you? else you'll die. I swallered a lot o' poison berries once and I was dead all one night arterwards . . . '

'Real dead?'

'Real dead,' Ben said. 'All one night.'

'What does it feel like to be dead?'

'Fust you git terrible belly ache,' Ben said, 'and then your head keeps going jimmity – jimmity – jimmity – bonk – bonk – bonk – clang – bang – jimmity – bonk – clang – bonk all the time.'

'Does it make you sick?'

'Sicking up all the time,' Ben said, 'and seeing old men dancing upside down on the bedroom wall and laughing at you – like my Uncle Perce does when he comes home from *The Unicorn*.'

'I don't want to be dead,' I said, 'I don't want to be dead.'

'Then don't eat no poison berries. You know what poison

berries look like, don't you?'

'No.'

'Some are red,' Ben said, 'and some are black. But all on 'em make you sick and give you belly ache and make your head jimmity – jimmity – bonk – clang – bonk – bang – jimmity – '

My blood felt cold, I felt like sobbing and above me where I lay face downwards under the blackberry hedge, giant stalks of cow parsnip stood like frozen white skeleton sentinels against the late summer sky.

'Why don't we start?' I said. I knew we had a long way to go; Ben said so.

Ben got his knife out and opened the stabber.

'I got to see if there's any spies fust,' Ben said. 'You stop here.'

'How long?'

'Till I git back,' Ben said. 'Don't you move and don't you shout and don't you show yourself and don't you eat no poison berries.'

'No,' I said. 'No.'

Ben flashed the knife so that the stabber pierced the blackberry shade.

'You know Ossy Turner?' he said.

'Yes,' I said. 'Yes.'

Ossy had a hare-lip and walked with one drawling foot and a crooked hand. I always felt awfully sorry for Ossy but Ben said:

'Ossy's like that because he come down here and dint look for spies fust – so they got him and done that to him.'

'Who did?'

Ben was crawling away on hairy knees, flashing the stabber in the sunlight, leaving me alone.

' "The Poison Ladies" ',' Ben said, 'what live down here. In that house I told you about. Them two old wimmin what we're goin' to see if we can see.'

Ben went crawling forward; the brown leather patches on his trousers seat vanished clean from my range of sight. I shut my eyes and lay down alone in dead blackberry leaves and tried to listen for skylarks singing. Whenever I was alone in the fields I listened for the sound of skylarks. The song always seemed to sparkle in the solitude.

But now it was nearly September. It was too late for skylarks and all I could hear was the simmering drone of grasshoppers among yellowing grasses, out in the sun.

It was fifty years before Ben came back. I knew quite well that it was fifty years; I counted every one of them.

'No footmarks,' Ben said.

'I didn't eat any poison berries. I didn't – '

'Let's have a look at your tongue!'

My tongue shot out like a frightened lizard. With big white eyes Ben glared down my throat and said:

'All right. We're going now. Hold your breath.'

'How far is it now?'

'Miles,' Ben said. 'Down the lane and past the shippen and over the brook and then up the lane and across the Akky Duck.'

I didn't know what the Akky Duck was; I thought it must be a bird.

'It's like bridges,' Ben said. 'It's dark underneath 'em where the water goes over.'

'Do the poison ladies live there?'

'They come jist arterwards,' Ben said. 'We hide under the Akky Duck and arter that you can see 'em squinting through the winders.'

The veins about my heart tied themselves in knots as I followed Ben out of the blackberry shade, over the fence, into the lane and past black bushes of sloe powderily bloomed with blue fruit in the sun.

Once I tried to draw level with Ben and walk beside him, just for company, but he turned the stabber on me sharply and said:

'You keep behind me. I'm leader. I know the way, see? I got to git there fust to see if it's all right, see? Else they might do to you what they did to old Ossy, see?'

'Yes, Ben. Yes, Ben. Yes, Ben. Yes, Ben.'

Not long after that we passed a place in the brook where sheep were washed. Ben said I was to look at the water and see how gold it was. That was because it was poison and you'd die if you washed your hands there. Just beyond it great elephant umbrellas of hemlock grew in lush wet shade and Ben said they were poison too.

'Keep in,' he kept saying. 'Keep in. Crouch down. We're coming to the Akky Duck.'

Soon we were crouching under the dark brick of the bridge. It was suddenly cold and the bricks dripped water. Ferns sprouted green fingers from crevices and Ben said there were snails as big as turnips there, with horns as long as bike-pumps.

'And snakes. And lizards. And rats. And Devil's Coach and Horses.'

'Are they poison too?'

'All on 'em. Everythink's poison down here.'

I wanted to hang on to Ben's coat tails and play horses, but Ben said no, he was going on ahead again to look for spies and that I'd got to wait and stand still and not breathe a word until he whistled a signal back to me.

So I stood under the Akky Duck all alone while Ben went out into the sunlight at the far end to look for spies. I didn't see any snails or lizards or snakes or Devil's Coach and Horses, but water dripped about me in long slow spits, splashing in the shadow.

When Ben whistled at last I jumped clean out of my skin and started running through black pools of water.

'Don't run, you wet ha'puth,' Ben said. 'They'll hear you. They got ears like old sows. They hang down to their shoulders.'

I think I must have shivered as I came out into sunlight, because Ben said:

'You ain't frit are you?'

'No,' I said. 'No, I'm not frit.'

'If you're frit,' Ben said, 'they'll know. Then they'll put both on us in the copper.'

'Why?' I said. 'Why?'

'To boil us up, you wet ha'puth!' Ben said: '*To boil us up.*'

'You said once they poisoned you.'

'So they do,' Ben said. 'Poison you fust, then boil you arterwards.'

Before I could speak again Ben was pointing ahead.

'There it is. That's where they live,' he said. 'That's the house.'

Fifty yards ahead stood a double-bayed house of red brick with a blue slate roof and cowls with foxes' tails on the chimneys. The cowls were black. Half the slates were off the roof and most of the glass was broken in the windows.

When we got a little nearer I could see there were plum trees in the garden, with ripe blue oval fruit shining in the sun. I could see an empty chicken run overgrown with grass and a big red earthenware pot with huge rhubarb leaves growing out of the top like inside-out umbrellas. It was hot now after the tunnel and everywhere the grasshoppers whirred.

I started to say that the house was empty but Ben said:

'Ah! That's what *you* think. That's what the old wimmen *want* you to think.'

'Why do they?'

'They want you to climb the fence and start gittin' the plums and then jist as you're gittin' 'em they spring out an' collar you.'

The veins about my heart tied themselves into tighter, colder knots as we crept along the fence on our hands and knees.

'Crouch down,' Ben kept whispering. 'Crouch down. Don't let 'em see you.'

Then we were in front of the house, in full view of the broken windows, the slateless rafters and the smokey cowls. The sun was on our backs and the light of it sharpened the splintered windows. The plums looked big and luscious now and you could see yellow wasps turning and shimmering madly about the trees.

'The plums are poison anyhow,' Ben said, 'even if they dint collar you. And even if you dint die o' poison the wasps'd sting you to death.'

All about the house, from the broken window sashes to the stiff black fox tails, there wasn't a single movement in the sun.

Then Ben was clutching my arm and whispering hoarsely and pointing upward.

'There they are. There's one on 'em now. Watching.'

'Where?' I said. 'Where?'

'Up at that window. On the left-hand side.'

Ben didn't know his right hand from his left hand and nor did I. He pointed with the hand he held his knife in and I stared at the right-hand upstairs window but there was nothing there.

'Can't you see her?' Ben said. 'She's got long white pigtails and you can see her big ears.'

I looked at all the windows, one by one, upstairs and down, but there was nothing to be seen except splintered holes in the glass, naked and white-edged in the sunlight.

'She don't have no teeth, this one,' Ben said, 'and her mouth's all green.'

I didn't dare tell Ben I couldn't see anything, but suddenly he grabbed my arm:

'And there's the other one!' he whispered. 'Downstairs. The one with yeller eyes.'

My heart curdled. I started shivering down the whole length of my spine.

'Big yeller eyes she's got,' Ben said. 'Big yeller eyes. Like brimstone.'

All the windows downstairs were empty too and the only yellow I could see was in the clouds of wasps whirling about the laden plum trees.

'Can't you see her?' Ben said. 'Can't you see her?'

'No.'

He turned and looked at me sharply, in derision.

'You'll never see 'em with your eyes wide open like that, you wet ha'porth. You gotta squint with 'em. Squint. Like this, see? Like owls do, see?'

Ben had his eyes all screwed up so that they were no more than dark slits.

'Owls can see in the dark,' he said. 'They can see what ain't there when we look. You know that, don't you?'

I knew that; my father had told me so. And suddenly I screwed up my eyes like an owl's too, just like Ben.

And when I looked at the house again it was just as Ben had said. I too could see the two old women at the windows, one upstairs and one down, the two old poison ladies, one with yellow eyes and the other with a green mouth and long white pigtails, both of them with awful ears, like sows.

'I can see them now, Ben,' I said, 'I can see them now.'

'Look out! They're coming!' Ben said. 'They're arter us!'

Then we were running, in terror, faster than wasps, under the Akky Duck, past the hemlock, the gold poison water, the shippen and the blue-black aisles of sloes. My breath was burning my chest and throat but my spine was chilled from the hairs of my neck downward and the knots round my heart coiled more and more tightly, deadly cold.

We didn't stop running until we were out in the big open field at the top of the lane. Then Ben started laughing and I was laughing too.

'We seen 'em!' Ben said. 'Both on 'em! They was there! We seen 'em! They was there!'

'We seen 'em!' I said. 'We seen 'em!'

Ben began turning somersaults in the grass and I tried to turn somersaults too. All the time we were laughing and flinging up our hands and shouting.

'I could see her yeller eyes!'

'And the other one's green mouth!'

'And the white pig-tails!'

'And their big ears!'

Suddenly a rook cackled sharply in the meadows below us, down where the hemlock grew. Ben looked back down the lane, startled, and I was startled too.

'Let's play horses,' Ben said. 'Let's gallop all the way home.'

'I'll be horse,' I said and in a second I was out in front, champing my bit, with Ben holding my coat tails, and a moment later we were away like a cold thin wind.

'We see the poison ladies!' Ben kept shouting. 'We see the ole poison ladies!'

'We see the poison ladies!' I echoed. 'We see the old poison ladies!'

'They chased us! They nearly got us!'

'They nearly got us!'

'I bet they don't cut their ole nails fer a million years.'

'I bet they don't cut their old nails for a million years.'

Everything Ben shouted I shouted too. When he laughed I laughed. What he believed I believed. He wasn't afraid and I wasn't afraid. I was only flying home like a wild wind.

When you are only four, seven is a hundred and five inches are a mile.

Smart Ice Cream

PAUL JENNINGS

WELL, I CAME top of the class again. One hundred out of one hundred for Maths. And one hundred out of one hundred for English. I'm just a natural brain, the best there is. There isn't one kid in the class who can come near me. Next to me they are all dumb.

Even when I was a baby I was smart. The day that I was born my mother started tickling me. 'Bub, bub bub,' she said.

'Cut it out, Mum,' I told her. 'That tickles.' She nearly fell out of bed when I said that. I was very advanced for my age.

Every year I win a lot of prizes: top of the class, top of the school, stuff like that. I won a prize for spelling when I was only three years old. I am a terrific speller. If you can say it, I can spell it. Nobody can trick me on spelling. I can spell every word there is.

Some kids don't like me; I know that for a fact. They say I'm a show off. I don't care. They are just jealous because they are not as clever as me. I'm good looking too. That's another reason why they are jealous.

Last week something bad happened. Another kid got one hundred out of one hundred for Maths too. That never happened before — no one has ever done as well as me. I am always first on my own. A kid called Jerome Dadian beat me. He must have cheated. I was sure he cheated. It had something to do with that ice cream. I was sure of it. I decided to find out what was going on; I wasn't going to let anyone pull a fast one on me.

It all started with the ice cream man, Mr Peppi. The old fool had a van which he parked outside the school. He sold ice cream, all different types. He had every flavour there is, and some that I had never heard of before.

He didn't like me very much. He told me off once. 'Go to the back of the queue,' he said. 'You pushed in.'

'Mind your own business, Pop,' I told him. 'Just hand over the ice cream.'

'No,' he said. 'I won't serve you unless you go to the back.'

I went round to the back of the van, but I didn't get in the queue. I took out a nail and made a long scratch on his rotten old van. He had just had it painted. Peppi came and had a look. Tears came into his eyes. 'You are a bad boy,' he said. 'One day you will get into trouble. You think you are smart. One day you will be too smart.'

I just laughed and walked off. I knew he wouldn't do anything. He was too soft-hearted. He was always giving free ice creams to kids that had no money. He felt sorry for poor people. The silly fool.

There were a lot of stories going round about that ice cream. People said that it was good for you. Some kids said that it made you better when you were sick. One of the teachers called it 'Happy Ice Cream'. I didn't believe it; it never made me happy.

All the same, there was something strange about it. Take Pimples Peterson for example. That wasn't his real name – I just called him that because he had a lot of pimples. Anyway, Peppi heard me calling Peterson 'Pimples'. 'You are a real mean boy,' he said. 'You are always picking on someone else, just because they are not like you.'

'Get lost, Peppi,' I said. 'Go and flog your ice cream somewhere else.'

Peppi didn't answer me. Instead he spoke to Pimples. 'Here, eat this,' he told him. He handed Peterson an ice cream. It was the biggest ice cream I had ever seen. It was coloured purple. Peterson wasn't too sure about it. He didn't think he had enough money for such a big ice cream.

'Go on,' said Mr Peppi. 'Eat it. I am giving it to you for

nothing. It will get rid of your pimples.'

I laughed and laughed. Ice cream doesn't get rid of pimples, it *gives* you pimples. Anyway, the next day when Peterson came to school he had no pimples. Not one. I couldn't believe it. The ice cream had cured his pimples.

There were some other strange things that happened too. There was a kid at the school who had a long nose. Boy, was it long. He looked like Pinocchio. When he blew it you could hear it a mile away. I called him 'Snozzle'. He didn't like being called Snozzle. He used to go red in the face when I said it, and that was every time that I saw him. He didn't say anything back – he was scared that I would punch him up.

Peppi felt sorry for Snozzle too. He gave him a small green ice cream every morning, for nothing. What a jerk. He never gave me a free ice cream.

You won't believe what happened but I swear it's true. Snozzle's nose began to grow smaller. Every day it grew a bit smaller. In the end it was just a normal nose. When it was the right size Peppi stopped giving him the green ice creams.

I made up my mind to put a stop to this ice cream business. Jerome Dadian had been eating ice cream the day he got one hundred for Maths. It must have been the ice cream making him smart. I wasn't going to have anyone doing as well as me. I was the smartest kid in the school, and that's the way I wanted it to stay. I wanted to get a look inside that ice cream van to find out what was going on.

I knew where Peppi kept his van at night – he left it in a small lane behind his house. I waited until about eleven o'clock at night. Then I crept out of the house and down to Peppi's van. I took a crowbar, a bucket of sand, a torch and some bolt cutters with me.

There was no one around when I reached the van. I sprang the door open with the crowbar and shone my torch around inside. I had never seen so many tubs of ice cream before. There was every flavour you could think of: there was apple and banana, cherry and mango, blackberry and watermelon and about fifty other flavours. Right at the end of the van were four bins with locks on them. I went over and had a look. It was just as I thought – these were his special flavours. Each one had writing on the top. This is what they said:

HAPPY ICE CREAM for cheering people up.

NOSE ICE CREAM for long noses.

PIMPLE ICE CREAM for removing pimples.

SMART ICE CREAM for smart alecs.

Now I knew his secret. That rat Dadian had been eating Smart Ice Cream; that's how he got one hundred for Maths. I knew there couldn't be anyone as clever as me. I decided to fix Peppi up once and for all. I took out the bolt cutters and cut the locks off the four bins; then I put sand into every bin in the van. Except for the Smart Ice Cream. I didn't put any sand in that.

I laughed to myself. Peppi wouldn't sell much ice cream now. Not unless he started a new flavour – Sand Ice Cream. I looked at the Smart Ice Cream. I decided to eat some; it couldn't do any harm. Not that I needed it – I was already about as smart as you could get. Anyway, I gave it a try. I ate the lot. Once I started I couldn't stop. It tasted good. It was delicious.

I left the van and went home to bed, but I couldn't sleep. To tell the truth, I didn't feel too good. So I decided to write this. Then if any funny business has been going on you people will know what happened. I think I have made a mistake. I don't think Dadian did get any Smart Ice Cream.

It iz the nekst day now. Somefing iz hapening to me. I don't feal quite az smart. I have bean trying to do a reel hard sum. It iz wun and wun. Wot duz wun and wun make? Iz it free or iz it for?

The Kitten

ALEXANDER REID

THE FEET WERE tramping directly towards her. In the hot darkness under the tarpaulin the cat cuffed a kitten to silence and listened intently.

She could hear the scruffling and scratching of hens about the straw-littered yard; the muffled grumbling of the turning churn in the dairy; the faint clink and jangle of harness from the stable – drowsy, comfortable, reassuring noises through which the clang of the iron-shod boots on the cobbles broke ominously.

The boots ground to a halt, and three holes in the cover, brilliant diamond-points of light, went suddenly black. Couching, the cat waited, then sneezed and drew back as the tarpaulin was thrown up and glaring white sunlight struck at her eyes.

She stood over her kittens, the fur of her back bristling and the pupils of her eyes narrowed to pin-points. A kitten mewed plaintively.

For a moment, the hired man stared stupidly at his discovery, then turned towards the stable and called harshly, 'Hi, Maister! Here a wee.'

A second pair of boots clattered across the yard, and the face of the farmer, elderly, dark and taciturn, turned down on the cats.

'So that's whaur she's been,' commented the newcomer slowly.

He bent down to count the kittens and the cat struck at him, scoring a red furrow across the back of his wrist. He caught her by the neck and flung her roughly aside. Mewing she came back and began to lick her kittens. The Master turned away.

'Get rid of them,' he ordered. 'There's ower mony cats aboot this place.'

'Aye, Maister,' said the hired man.

Catching the mother he carried her, struggling and swearing, to the stable, flung her in, and latched the door. From the loft he secured an old potato sack and with this in his hand returned to the kittens.

There were five, and he noticed their tigerish markings without comprehending as, one by one, he caught them and thrust them into the bag. They were old enough to struggle, spitting, clawing and biting at his fingers.

Throwing the bag over his shoulder he stumped down the hill to the burn, stopping twice on the way to wipe the sweat that trickled down his face and neck, rising in beads between the roots of his lint-white hair.

Behind him, the buildings of the farm-steading shimmered in the heat. The few trees on the slope raised dry, brittle branches towards a sky bleached almost white. The smell of the farm, mingled with peat-reek, dung, cattle, milk, and the dark tang of the soil, was strong in his nostrils, and when he halted there was no sound but his own breathing and the liquid burbling of the burn.

Throwing the sack on the bank, he stepped into the stream. The water was low, and grasping a great boulder in the bed of the burn he strained to lift it, intending to make a pool.

He felt no reluctance at performing the execution. He had no feelings about the matter. He had drowned kittens before. He would drown them again.

Panting with his exertion, the hired man cupped water between his hands and dashed it over his face and neck in a glistening shower. Then he turned to the sack and its prisoners.

He was in time to catch the second kitten as it struggled out of the bag. Thrusting it back and twisting the mouth of the sack close, he went after the other. Hurrying on the sun-browned grass, treacherous as ice, he slipped and fell headlong, but grasped the runaway in his outflung hand.

It writhed round immediately and sank needle-sharp teeth into his thumb so that he grunted with pain and shook it from him. Unhurt, it fell by a clump of whins and took cover beneath them.

The hired man, his stolidity shaken by frustration, tried to follow. The whins were thick and, scratched for his pains, he drew back, swearing flatly, without colour or passion.

Stooping, he could see the eyes of the kitten staring at him from the shadows under the whins. Its back was arched, its fur erect, its mouth open, and its thin lips drawn back over its tiny white teeth.

The hired man saw, again without understanding, the beginnings of tufts on the flattened ears. In his dull mind he felt a dark resentment at this creature which defied him. Rising, he passed his hand up his face in heavy thought, then slithering down to the stream, he began to gather stones. With an armful of small water-washed pebbles he returned to the whins.

First he strove to strike at the kitten from above. The roof of the whins was matted and resilient. The stones could not penetrate it. He flung straight then – to maim or kill – but the angle was difficult and only one missile reached its mark, rebounding from the ground and striking the kitten a glancing blow on the shoulder.

Kneeling, his last stone gone, the hired man watched, the red in his face deepening and thin threads of crimson rising in the whites of his eyes as the blood mounted to his head. A red glow of anger was spreading through his brain. His mouth worked and twisted to an ugly rent.

'Wait – wait,' he cried hoarsely, and, turning, ran heavily up the slope to the trees. He swung his whole weight on a low-hanging branch, snapping it off with a crack like a gunshot.

Seated on the warm, short turf, the hired man prepared his weapon, paring at the end of the branch till the point was sharp as a dagger. When it was ready he knelt on his left knee and swung the branch to find the balance. The kitten was almost caught.

The savage lance-thrust would have skewered its body as a trout is spiked on the beak of a heron, but the point, slung too low, caught in a fibrous root and snapped off short. Impotently the man jabbed with his broken weapon while the kitten retreated disdainfully to the opposite fringe of the whins.

In the slow-moving mind of the hired man the need to destroy the kitten had become an obsession. Intent on this victim, he forgot the others abandoned by the burn side; forgot the passage of time, and the hard labour of the day behind him. The kitten, in his distorted mind, had grown to a monstrous thing, centring all the frustrations of a brutish existence. He craved to kill . . .

But so far the honours lay with the antagonist.

In a sudden flash of fury the man made a second bodily assault on the whins and a second time retired defeated.

He sat down on the grass to consider the next move as the first breath of the breeze wandered up the hill. As though that were the signal, in the last moments of the sun, a lark rose, close at hand, and mounted the sky on the flood of its own melody.

The man drank in the coolness thankfully, and, taking a pipe from his pocket, lit the embers of tobacco in the bowl. He flung the match from him, still alight, and a dragon's tongue of amber flame ran over the dry grass before the breeze, reached a bare patch of sand and flickered out. Watching it, the hired man knitted his brows and remembered the heather burning, and mountain hares that ran before the scarlet terror. And he looked at the whins.

The first match blew out in the freshening wind, but at the second the bush burst into crackling flame.

The whins were alight on the leeward side and burned slowly against the wind. Smoke rose thickly, and sparks and lighted shivers of wood sailed off on the wind to light new fires on the grass of the hillside.

Coughing as the pungent smoke entered his lungs, the man circled the clump till the fire was between him and the farm. He could see the kitten giving ground slowly before the flame. He thought for a moment of lighting this side of the clump also and trapping it between two fires; took his matches from his pocket, hesitated, and replaced them. He could wait.

Slowly, very slowly, the kitten backed towards him. The wind fought for it, delaying, almost holding the advance of the fire through the whins.

Showers of sparks leaped up from the bushes that crackled and spluttered as they burned, but louder than the crackling of the whins, from the farm on the slope of the hill, came another noise – the clamour of voices. The hired man walked clear of the smoke that obscured his view and stared up the hill.

The thatch of the farmhouse, dry as tinder, was aflare.

Gaping, he saw the flames spread to the roof of the byre, to the stables; saw the farmer running the horses to safety, and heard the thunder of hooves as the scared cattle, turned loose, rushed from the yard. He saw a roof collapse in an uprush of smoke and sparks, while a kitten, whose sire was a wild cat, passed out of the whins unnoticed and took refuge in a deserted burrow.

From there, with cold defiant eyes, it regarded the hired man steadfastly.

Wolf Alone

JAN NEEDLE

ON THE DAY that the wolf returned, he sensed that it was the end. As he tore his matted pelt through the thorn bushes to the lair he smelled the smell of dog and man. He scented blood, and he scented coldness. The lair was empty.

As he reached the heart of the bushes, the alien scents were overwhelming. Axe and sword marks were fresh on the shattered branches. One whole side of the lair had been cut and torn aside, exposing it to the light. Even men and clumsy horses had been able to approach. There was nothing left of the cubs, save bloodstained fur and some shards of bone. The earth was soaked in blood.

The wolf did not know what had happened, but he knew the she-wolf had not been there. If she had been, there would have been other bones and fur, of hounds, and horses, even men. Either she had been out hunting food, or she had been killed beforehand. He had been gone for days.

For some minutes, the wolf stood amid the wreckage of the lair, his nostrils quivering in the violent mixture of scents. Everything was cold, there was no lingering warmth. The carnage had been some hours ago. The wolf shivered suddenly, bristling the grey-brown fur at his neck. He picked his way through the broken thorn branches to a pathway in the forest. After searching for some minutes for the scent of the she-wolf, he gave it up. The smell of man was dominant. Of man, and horse, and hound. The wolf began to follow.

Normally, he would not have mated with this particular

she-wolf, and that was part of the mystery. The she-wolf was young, and fit, and fertile. He himself was old, and now – after his long and fruitless journey – he was weakened, and badly lame in one hind leg. He had tried to kill a pig, a wild sow, many miles to the south, and she had bested him in speed. When he had followed – recklessly, but with the necessity to eat tearing at his innards – her mate, a handsome boar, had come upon them. As the wolf had fled, the boar had charged. He had been knocked sideways, his leg slashed by a tusk, and had been lucky to escape alive.

The wolf had mated with the she-wolf for the same reason that he had made his journey. It was a strange necessity, brought about by the fortunes of the pack. For the pack, when the mating had taken place, had dwindled to a tiny handful, and despite his age he was the only male. In the days that followed, the other wolves had died as well. The remnants of the pack had separated, and had soon been killed. The hunters were like a scourge, they bore down with their dogs, and their cross-bows and their spears, and they raged throughout the forest and they killed. Not just wolves alone. In the years that he had lived, the wolf had seen many animals killed or driven from the land. The wild pig he had tried to eat, in the south, had been – to him – a rarity. In the area where he lived, the pigs had died out long ago.

The wolf was old – but not too old to mate – because he was the craftiest, and the strongest, of the males. He had been the leader for a great time, and his experience alone enabled him to outwit the hunters. Many times he had been scented by the hounds, many times he had outwitted them. He had never killed a man, but he had killed their dogs, and their domestic animals. He recognized men as mighty hunters, and he feared them. In the end, they had destroyed his pack.

After the litter was born, and had achieved enough strength to be left while the she-wolf foraged, the wolf had set out on his journey. He had nuzzled the she-wolf, and licked her face, and left. She knew, as well as he, that something must happen. The cubs were healthy, they were strong. But the pack was finished. Either new blood must come to them, or they must find new blood. He licked her face and left.

In the northern part of Wales, where the wolf lived, there were vast tracts of woodland, both light and scattered copses and dense and gloomy forests. There were mountains also, and rushing, pure rivers. Not many human beings, with the settlements small and widely separated. They farmed sheep in the main, with some small herds of cattle here and there. But although the beasts of prey were not in evidence, the domestic animals were guarded closely. By day they were watched over by men and boys with slings and longbows on the hillsides. By night they were in stone folds, also closely watched. Perhaps the beasts of prey were men from other settlements, or wandering bands of robbers. For of wolves and other predators, there were none. It was as if a plague had come upon the land. Only wildcats came within his scent, and that not often.

He travelled for some days – or rather, mainly, nights – and he travelled south and east. He explored the mountains of Wales, then trekked towards the border forests and the plains of England. He moved through Cheshire and the Wirral, and he described a huge circle back towards the lands his pack had always colonized. He saw no wolves. When he returned to the lair he was many pounds lighter, and hungry. All wildlife had diminished terribly; the scourge had travelled far and wide. Only the smaller forms were general now, and most of them were well beyond his reach. He was too slow. He was too big and clumsy.

Today, the trail he followed was broad and fresh. It was not by scent alone that he went, for the visible signs were many. There had been several hunters, and the way they had broken through the undergrowth was as clear to him as would have been a track. At one stage there was a bigger broken space, as if another animal had been surrounded and set upon. The wolf sniffed around it carefully, and once he thought he found a trace of wolf. But the scents were too many, too strong. He could not be sure.

It was in the middle of the afternoon that he reached the thinning fringes of the forest, and for some time past the wolf had felt another instinct murmuring in his brain. Somehow, he knew, another hunt was up. Somehow, he knew, he would soon find signs of man the predator, preparing to make a foray to the woodland. The old wolf paused, and studied the ground, the trees, the sky. It was a warm day, a cloudless, sunny day in the autumn of the year. Although he could hear nothing but the forest sounds, the sense was strong upon him. Another hunt was up.

The wolf began to lope through the last vestiges of the forest. At the edge, he mounted a small hillock and looked down across the plain. There were rich green fields, divided in places, and tilled. There was a small settlement, huddled cottages with smoke blowing from their fires. Behind them, massive and grey, was the castle where the hunters had their lair. The wolf was right. Before the castle was a mass of them. Men and horses, wolfhounds huge and grey.

The wolf waited for an age before he turned into the forest once more. He stood upon the hillock as the hunt turned itself from a coloured jumble to a column of clear determination. He watched as the hounds were whipped into shape, then unleashed to spread before the horses like a tide. The wind was blowing from them in his direction, and the smell of them was powerful and keen. But his instincts now were dulled. No desperate fear arose within him, to make him turn and flee. He stood and watched. He could see their dripping mouths, their lolling tongues. He could hear them panting, eager and ferocious. The hooves of the horses rumbled in his ears, their leathers creaked. The men shouted, gaily.

When the dogs finally saw him, it caused confusion in their ranks. A few stopped, tumbling over themselves. For he was standing there, unmoving. It was unknown. There was a noise of disorder, sharp and sudden, before their voices gave a bay of certainty, the savage roar of bloodlust. They spread across the green earth like a cancer, then arrowed for the spot. In that split-second, the wolf was gone.

He ran in a straight line, and he ran faster than he had run for days. He burst through a shallow stream to hide his scent, then continued in a single direction, not even looking to left or right. The damaged leg caused pain, but he overrode it. The wolf was running blind, he was in flight. He smashed through bush and briar, he leapt over log and gully. He sped deep into the heart of the forest.

The dogs soon found his scent, but the way he took was murderous. By the time the wolf broke into a clearing, they were several minutes behind him. In the clearing, the wolf stopped dead. He stood there panting, with foam and saliva running from his jaws. His sides were heaving. In front of him was a house.

It was totally unexpected, and the wolf became confused. Running blind, his instinct had been to seek the heart, the dark centre of the forest where men, perhaps, could never tread. He knew this house, of course, he had avoided it of old. Now here he was. As he stood, bracing his nerves and muscles for another desperate plunge, a human being came into his sight.

Now the wolf froze. The human being was a child, a plump, round morsel of a child, about as tall as his own shoulder, smaller than his panting head. It came round the side of the house, and gave a little cry at the sight of him. It was a cry of pleasure, not of threat, there was no fear in it. As the wolf stood, the child began to run towards him, a joyful, stumbling run. It stretched out one chubby hand as it approached, and it was gambolling like a cub.

Like a cub. But this was no wolf cub, it was the child of man. This plump, defenceless creature was the enemy. It would grow up to kill him, like the rest. It would denude the forest and destroy the beasts. The wolves would go, the wildcats and the boars. Until there was nothing. Nothing that was not a slave of man. It was the scourge.

The child stopped in front of the wolf, and laughed at him. It was food as well. One mouthful, torn away before the flight, would give him strength. The gushing blood would slake his thirst, send energy to his quivering muscle instantly. It would save his life, perhaps.

As the child reached out a hand to him, the smell of the hounds flooded the senses of the wolf. He jumped sideways, knocking the child to the ground. The leading hounds appeared in the undergrowth, their eyes red, almost screaming now with the lust to kill. Beside him, the child would be torn to pieces with the wolf, they would not discriminate. The wolf loped across the grass and bounded on to the wall around the cottage. From the wall he leapt on to the roof of a low outhouse. There, as the hounds clamoured in a savage boiling below him and the men on horses appeared, he turned at bay.

A crossbow bolt despatched him, entering between his eyes and smashing his skull to pieces. Before he was struck, the wolf had seen the she-wolf's head held proudly high, and stuck upon a lance. Neither he nor the huntsmen knew it, but he was the last wild wolf in Britain. He was the last.

The Banana Tree

JAMES BERRY

IN THE HOURS the hurricane stayed, its presence made everybody older. It made Mr Bass see that not only people and animals and certain valuables were of most importance to be saved.

From its very build-up the hurricane meant to show it was merciless, unstoppable, and with its might it changed landscapes.

All day the Jamaican sun didn't come out. Then, ten minutes before, there was a swift shower of rain that raced by and was gone like some urgent messenger-rush of wind. And, again, everything went back to that quiet, that unnatural quiet. It was as if trees crouched quietly in fear. As if, too, birds knew they should shut up. A thick and low black cloud had covered the sky and shadowed everywhere, and made it seem like night was coming on. And the cloud deepened. Its deepening spread more and more over the full stretch of the sea.

The doom-laden afternoon had the atmosphere of Judgement Day for everybody in all the districts about. Everybody knew the hour of disaster was near. Warnings printed in bold lettering had been put up at post offices, police stations, schoolyard entrances and in clear view on shop walls in village squares.

Carrying children and belongings, people hurried in files and in scattered groups, headed for the big, strong and safe community buildings. In Canerise Village, we headed for the schoolroom. Loaded with bags and cases, with bundles and lidded baskets, individuals carrying or leading an animal, parents shrieking for children to stay at their heels, we arrived there. And, looking round, anyone would think the whole of Canerise was here in this vast super barn of a noisy chattering schoolroom.

With violent gusts and squalls the storm broke. Great rushes, huge bulky rushes, of wind struck the building in heavy repeated thuds, shaking it over and over, and carrying on.

Families were huddled together on the floor. People sang, sitting on benches, desks, anywhere there was room. Some people knelt in loud prayer. Among the refugees' noises a goat bleated, a hen fluttered or cackled, a dog whined.

Mr Jetro Bass was sitting on a soap-box. His broad back leaned on the blackboard against the wall. Mrs Imogene Bass, largely pregnant, looked a midget beside him. Their children were sitting on the floor. The eldest boy, Gustus, sat farthest from his father. Altogether, the children's heads made seven different levels of height around the parents. Mr Bass forced a reassuring smile. His toothbrush moustache moved about a bit as he said, 'The storm's bad, chil'run. Really bad. But it'll blow off. It'll spen' itself out. It'll kill itself.'

Except for Gustus, all the faces of the children turned up with subdued fear and looked at their father as he spoke.

'Das true wha' Pappy say,' Mrs Bass said. 'The good Lord wohn gi' we more than we can bear.'

Mr Bass looked at Gustus. He stretched fully through the sitting children and put a lumpy, blistery hand – though a huge hand – on the boy's head, almost covering it. The boy's clear brown eyes looked straight and unblinkingly into his father's face. 'Wha's the matter, bwoy?' his dad asked.

He shook his head. 'Nothin', Pappy.'

'Wha' mek you say "not'n"? I sure somet'in' bodder you, Gustus. You not a bwoy who fright'n easy. Is not the hurricane wha' bodder you? Tell Pappy.'

'Is nothin'.'

'You're a big bwoy now. Gustus – you nearly thirteen. You strong. You very useful fo' you' age. You good as mi right han'. I depen' on you. But this afternoon – earlier – in the rush, when we so well push to move befo' storm brok', you couldn' rememba a t'ting! Not one t'ing! Why so? Wha' on you' mind? Yo 'arbourin' t'ings from me, Gustus?'

Gustus opened his mouth to speak, but closed it again. He knew his father was proud of how well he had grown. To strengthen him he had always given him 'last milk' straight from the cow in the mornings. He was thankful. But to him his strength was only proven in the number of wickets he could take for his cricket team. The boy's lips trembled. What's the good of tellin' when Pappy don' like cricket. He only get vex an' say it's Satan's game for idle hands! He twisted his head and looked away. 'I'm 'arbourin' nothin', Pappy.'

'Gustus . . .'

At that moment a man called, 'Mr Bass!' He came up quickly. 'Got a hymn book, Mr Bass? We want you to lead us singing.'

The people were sitting with bowed heads, humming a song. As the repressed singing grew louder and louder it sounded mournful in the room. Mr Bass shuffled, looking round as if he wished to back out of the suggestion. But his rich voice and singing-leadership were too famous. Mrs Bass already had the hymn-book in her hand and she pushed it on her husband. He took it, and began turning the leaves as he moved towards the centre of the room.

Immediately, Mr Bass was surrounded. He started with a resounding chant over the heads of everybody. 'Abide wid me, fast fall da eventide . . .' He joined the singing, but broke off to recite the other line. 'Da darkness deepen, Lord wid me abide . . .' Again, before the last long-drawn note faded from the deeply-stirred voices, Mr Bass intoned musically, 'When odder 'elpers fail, and comfats flee . . .'

In this manner he fired inspiration into the singing of hymn after hymn. The congregation swelled their throats and their mixed voices filled the room, pleading to heaven from the depths of their hearts. But the wind outside mocked viciously. It screamed. It whistled. It smashed everywhere up.

Mrs Bass had tightly closed her eyes, singing and swaying in the centre of the children who nestled round her. But Gustus was by himself. He had his elbows on his knees and his hands blocking his ears. He had his own worries.

What's the good of Pappy asking all those questions when he treat him so bad. He's the only one in the family without a pair of shoes! Because he's a big boy he dohn need anythin' an' must do all the work. He can't stay at school in the evenings an' play cricket because there's work to do at home. He can't have no outings with the other children because he has no shoes. An' now when he was to sell his bunch of bananas an' buy shoes so he can go out with his cricket team, the hurricane is going to blow it down.

It was true: the root of the banana was his 'navel string'. After his birth the umbilical cord was dressed with castor oil and sprinkled with nutmeg and buried, with the banana tree planted over it for him. When he was nine days old the Nana midwife had taken him out into the open for the first time. She had held the infant proudly and walked the twenty-five yards that separated the house from the kitchen, and at the back showed him his tree. ''Memba w'en you grow up,' her toothless mouth had said, 'It's you nable strings feedin' you tree, the same way it feed you from you mudder.'

Refuse from the kitchen made the plant flourish out of all proportion. But the rich soil around it was loose. Each time the tree gave a shoot, the bunch would be too heavy for the soil to support; so it crashed to the ground, crushing the tender fruit. This time, determined that his banana must reach the market, Gustus had supported his tree with eight props. And watching it night and morning it had become very close to him. Often he had seriously thought of moving his bed to its root.

Muffled cries, and the sound of blowing noses, now mixed with the singing. Delayed impact of the disaster was happening. Sobbing was everywhere. Quickly the atmosphere became sodden with the wave of weeping outbursts. Mrs Bass's pregnant belly heaved. Her younger children were upset and cried, 'Mammy, mammy, mammy . . .'

Realising that his family, too, was overwhelmed by the surrounding calamity, Mr Bass bustled over to them. Because their respect for him bordered fear, his presence quietened all immediately. He looked round. 'Where's Gustus! Imogene . . . where's Gustus!'

'He was 'ere, Pappy,' she replied, drying her eyes. 'I dohn know when he get up.'

Briskly, Mr Bass began combing the schoolroom to find his boy. He asked; no one had seen Gustus. He called. There was no answer. He tottered, lifting his heavy boots over heads, fighting his way to the jalousie. He opened it and his eyes gleamed up and down the road, but saw nothing of him. In despair Mr Bass gave one last thunderous shout: 'Gustus!' Only the wind sneered.

By this time Gustus was half-way on the mile journey to their house. The lone figure in the raging wind and shin-deep road-flood was tugging, snapping and pitching branches out of his path. His shirt was fluttering from his back like a boat-sail. And a leaf was fastened to his cheek. But the belligerent wind was merciless. It bellowed into his ears and drummed a deafening commotion. As he grimaced and covered his ears he was forcefully slapped against a coconut tree trunk that laid across the road.

When his eyes opened, his round face was turned up to a festered sky. Above the tormented trees a zinc sheet writhed, twisted and somersaulted in the tempestuous flurry. Leaves of all shapes and sizes were whirling and diving like attackers around the zinc sheet. As Gustus turned to get up, a bullet-drop of rain struck his temple. He shook his head, held grimly to the tree trunk and struggled to his feet.

Where the road was clear, he edged along the bank. Once, when the wind staggered him, he recovered with his legs wide apart. Angrily, he stretched out his hands with clenched fists and shouted: 'I almos' hol' you dat time . . . come solid like dat again an' we fight like man an' man!'

When Gustus approached the river he had to cross, it was flooded and blocked beyond recognition. Pressing his chest against the gritty road-bank the boy closed his weary eyes on the brink of the spating river. The wrecked footbridge had become the harbouring fort for all the debris, branches and monstrous tree-trunks which the river swept along its course. The river was still swelling. More accumulation arrived each moment, ramming and pressing the bridge. Under pressure it was cracking and shifting minutely towards a turbulent forty-foot fall.

Gustus had seen it! A feeling of dismay paralysed him, reminding him of his foolish venture. He scraped his cheek on the bank looking back. But how can he go back. He has no strength to go back. His house is nearer than the school. An' Pappy will only strap him for nothin' . . . for nothin' . . . no shoes, nothin' when the hurricane is gone.

With trembling fingers he tied up the remnants of his shirt. He made a bold step and the wind half-lifted him, ducking him in the muddy flood. He sank to his neck. Floating leaves, sticks, coconut husks, dead ratbats and all manner of feathered creatures and refuse surrounded him. Forest vines under the water entangled him. But he struggled desperately until he clung to the laden bridge, and climbed up among leafless branches.

His legs were bruised and bore deep scratches, but steadily he moved up on the slimy pile. He felt like a man at sea, in the heart of a storm, going up the mast of a ship. He rested his feet on a smooth log that stuck to the water-splashed heap like a black torso. As he strained up for another grip the torso came to life and leaped from under his feet. Swiftly sliding down, he grimly clutched some brambles.

The urgency of getting across became more frightening, and he gritted his teeth and dug his toes into the debris, climbing with maddened determination. But a hard gust of wind slammed the wreck, pinning him like a motionless lizard. For a minute the boy was stuck there, panting, swelling his naked ribs.

He stirred again and reached the top. He was sliding over a breadfruit limb when a flutter startled him. As he looked and saw the clean-head crow and glassy-eyed owl close together, there was a powerful jolt. Gustus flung himself into the air and fell in the expanding water on the other side. When he surfaced, the river had dumped the entire wreckage into the gurgling gully. For once the wind helped. It blew him to land.

Gustus was in a daze when he reached his house. Mud and rotten leaves covered his head and face, and blood caked around a gash on his chin. He bent down, shielding himself behind a tree-stump whose white heart was a needly splinter; murdered by the wind.

He could hardly recognise his yard. The terrorised trees that stood were writhing in turmoil. Their thatched house had collapsed like an open umbrella that was given a heavy blow. He looked the other way and whispered, 'Is still dere! Dat's a miracle . . . Dat's a miracle.'

Dodging the wind, he staggered from tree to tree until he got to his own tormented banana tree. Gustus hugged the tree. 'My nable string!' he cried. 'My nable string! I know you would stan' up to it, I know you would.'

The bones of the tree's stalky leaves were broken, and the wind lifted them and harassed them. And over Gustus's head the heavy fruit swayed and swayed. The props held the tree, but they were squeaking and slipping. And around the plant the roots stretched and trembled, gradually surfacing under loose earth.

With the rags of his wet shirt flying off his back, Gustus was down busily on his knees, bracing, pushing, tightening the props. One by one he was adjusting them until a heavy rush of wind knocked him to the ground. A prop fell on him, but he scrambled to his feet and looked up at the thirteen-hand bunch of bananas. 'My good tree,' he bawled, 'hol' yo' fruit . . . keep it to yo' heart like a mudder savin' her baby! Dohn let the wicked wind t'row you to the groun' . . . even if it t'row me to the groun'. I will not leave you.'

But several attempts to replace the prop were futile. The force of the wind against his weight was too much for him. He thought of a rope to lash the tree to anything, but it was difficult to make his way into the kitchen, which, separate from the house, was still standing. The invisible hand of the wind tugged, pushed and forcefully restrained him. He got down and crawled on his belly into the earth-floor kitchen. As he showed himself with the rope, the wind tossed him, like washing on the line, against his tree.

The boy was hurt! He looked crucified against the tree. The spike of the wind was slightly withdrawn. He fell, folded on the ground. He lay there unconscious. And the wind had no mercy for him. It shoved him, poked him, and molested his clothes like muddy newspaper against the tree.

As darkness began to move in rapidly, the wind grew more vicious and surged a mighty gust which struck the resisting kitchen. It was heaved to the ground in a rubbled pile. The brave wooden hut had been shielding the banana tree, but in its death-fall missed it by inches. The wind charged again and the soft tree gurgled – the fruit was torn from it and plunged to the ground.

The wind was less fierce when Mr Bass and a searching-party arrived with lanterns. Because the bridge was washed away, the hazardous roundabout journey had badly impeded them.

Talks about safety were mockery to the anxious father. Relentlessly he searched. In the darkness his great voice echoed everywhere, calling for his boy. He was wrenching and ripping through the house wreckage when suddenly he vaguely remembered how the boy had been fussing with the banana tree. Desperate, the man struggled from the ruins, flagging the lantern he carried.

The flickering light above his head showed Mr Bass the forlorn and pitiful banana tree. There it stood, shivering and twitching like a propped-up man with lacerated throat and dismembered head. Half of the damaged fruit rested on Gustus. The father hesitated. But when he saw a feeble wink of the boy's eyelids he flung himself to the ground. His bristly chin rubbed the child's face while his unsteady hand ran all over his body. 'My bwoy!' he murmured. 'Mi hurricane bwoy! The Good Lord save you . . . Why you do this? Why you do this?'

'I did wahn buy mi shoes, Pappy. I . . . I cahn go anywhere 'cause I have no shoes . . . I didn' go to school outing at the factory. I didn' go to Government House. I didn' go to Ol' Fort in town.'

Mr Bass sank into the dirt and stripped himself of his heavy boots. He was about lacing them to the boy's feet when the onlooking men prevented him. He tied the boots together and threw them over his shoulder.

Gustus's broken arm was strapped to his side as they carried him away. Mr Bass stroked his head and asked how he felt. Only then, grief swelled inside him and he wept.

Charles

SHIRLEY JACKSON

THE DAY LAURIE started kindergarten he renounced corduroy overalls with bibs and began wearing blue jeans with a belt; I watched him go off the first morning with the older girl next door, seeing clearly that an era of my life was ended, my sweet-voiced nursery-school tot replaced by a long-trousered, swaggering character who forgot to stop at the corner and wave goodbye to me.

He came home the same way, the front door slamming open, his cap on the floor, and the voice suddenly became raucous shouting, 'Isn't anybody *here?*'

At lunch he spoke insolently to his father, spilled Jannie's milk and remarked that his teacher said that we were not to take the name of the Lord in vain.

'How was school today?' I asked, elaborately casual.

'All right,' he said.

'Did you learn anything?' his father asked.

Laurie regarded his father coldly. 'I didn't learn nothing,' he said.

'Anything,' I said. 'Didn't learn anything.'

'The teacher spanked a boy, though,' Laurie said, addressing his bread and butter. 'For being fresh,' he added with his mouth full.

'What did he do?' I asked. 'Who was it?'

Laurie thought. 'It was Charles,' he said. 'He was fresh. The teacher spanked him and made him stand in a corner. He was awfully fresh.'

'What did he do?' I asked again, but Laurie slid off his chair, took a cookie, and left, while his father was still saying, 'See here, young man.'

The next day Laurie remarked at lunch, as soon as he sat down, 'Well, Charles was bad again today.' He grinned enormously and said, 'Today Charles hit the teacher.'

'Good heavens,' I said, mindful of the Lord's name. 'I suppose he got spanked again?'

'He sure did,' Laurie said. 'Look up,' he said to his father.

'What?' his father said, looking up.

'Look down,' Laurie said. 'Look at my thumb. Gee, you're dumb.' He began to laugh insanely.

'Why did Charles hit the teacher?' I asked quickly.

'Because she tried to make him colour with red crayons,' Laurie said. 'Charles wanted to colour with green crayons so he hit the teacher and she spanked him and said nobody play with Charles but everybody did.'

The third day – it was Wednesday of the first week – Charles bounced a seesaw onto the head of a little girl and made her bleed and the teacher made him stay inside all during recess. Thursday Charles had to stand in a corner during storytime because he kept pounding his feet on the floor. Friday Charles was deprived of blackboard privileges because he threw chalk.

On Saturday I remarked to my husband, 'Do you think kindergarten is too unsettling for Laurie? All this toughness and bad grammar, and this Charles boy sounds like such a bad influence.'

'It'll be all right,' my husband said reassuringly. 'Bound to be people like Charles in the world. Might as well meet them now as later.'

On Monday Laurie came home late, full of news. 'Charles,' he shouted as he came up the hill; I was waiting anxiously on the front steps; 'Charles,' Laurie yelled all the way up the hill, 'Charles was bad again.'

'Come right in,' I said, as soon as he came close enough. 'Lunch is waiting.'

'You know what Charles did?' he demanded, following me through the door. 'Charles yelled so in school they sent a boy in from first grade to tell the teacher she had to make Charles keep quiet, and so Charles had to stay after school. And so all the children stayed to watch him.'

'What did he do?' I asked.

'He just sat there,' Laurie said, climbing into his chair at the table. 'Hi Pop, y'old dust mop.'

'Charles had to stay after school today,' I told my husband. 'Everyone stayed with him.'

'What does this Charles look like?' my husband asked Laurie. 'What's his other name?'

'He's bigger than me,' Laurie said. 'And he doesn't have any rubbers and he doesn't ever wear a jacket.'

Monday night was the first Parent-Teachers meeting, and only the fact that Jannie had a cold kept me from going; I wanted passionately to meet Charles' mother. On Tuesday Laurie remarked suddenly, 'Our teacher had a friend come see her in school today.'

'Charles' mother?' my husband and I asked simultaneously.

'Naaah,' Laurie said scornfully. 'It was a man who came and made us do exercises. Look.' He climbed down from his chair and squatted down and touched his toes. 'Like this,' he said. He got solemnly back into his chair and said, picking up his fork, 'Charles didn't even *do* exercises.'

'That's fine,' I said heartily. 'Didn't Charles want to do exercises?'

'Naaah,' Laurie said. 'Charles was so fresh to the teacher's friend he wasn't *let* do exercises.'

'Fresh again?' I said.

'He kicked the teacher's friend,' Laurie said. 'The teacher's friend told Charles to touch his toes like I just did and Charles kicked him.'

'What are they going to do about Charles, do you suppose?' Laurie's father asked him.

Laurie shrugged elaborately. 'Throw him out of the school, I guess,' he said.

Wednesday and Thursday were routine; Charles yelled during story hour and hit a boy in the stomach and made him cry. On Friday Charles stayed after school again and so did all the other children.

With the third week of kindergarten Charles was an institution in our family; Jannie was being a Charles when she cried all afternoon; Laurie did a Charles when he filled his wagon full of mud and pulled it through the kitchen; even my husband, when he caught his elbow in the telephone cord and pulled telephone, ash tray, and a bowl of flowers off the table, said, after the first minute, 'Looks like Charles.'

During the third and fourth weeks there seemed to be a reformation in Charles; Laurie reported grimly at lunch on Thursday of the third week, 'Charles was so good today the teacher gave him an apple.'

'What?' I said, and my husband added warily, 'You mean Charles?'

'Charles,' Laurie said. 'He gave the crayons around and he picked up the books afterward and the teacher said he was her helper.'

'What happened?' I asked incredulously.

'He was her helper, that's all,' Laurie said, and shrugged.

'Can this be true, about Charles?' I asked my husband that night. 'Can something like this happen?'

'Wait and see,' my husband said cynically. 'When you've got a Charles to deal with, this may mean he's only plotting.'

He seemed to be wrong. For over a week Charles was the teacher's helper; each day he handed things out and he picked things up; no-one had to stay after school.

'The PTA meeting's next week again,' I told my husband one evening. 'I'm going to find Charles' mother there.'

'Ask her what happened to Charles,' my husband said. 'I'd like to know.'

On Friday of that week things were back to normal. 'You know what Charles did today?' Laurie demanded at the lunch table, in a voice slightly awed. 'He told a little girl to say a word and she said it and the teacher washed her mouth out with soap and Charles laughed.'

'What word?' his father asked unwisely, and Laurie said, 'I'll have to whisper it to you, it's so bad.' He got down off his chair and went around to his father. His father bent his head down and Laurie whispered joyfully. His father's eyes widened.

'Did Charles tell the little girl to say *that*?' he asked respectfully.

'She said it *twice*,' Laurie said. 'Charles told her to say it *twice*.'

'What happened to Charles?' my husband asked.

'Nothing,' Laurie said. 'He was passing out the crayons.'

Monday morning Charles abandoned the little girl and said the evil word himself three or four times, getting his mouth washed out with soap each time. He also threw chalk.

My husband came to the door with me that evening as I set out for the PTA meeting. 'Invite her over for a cup of tea after the meeting,' he said. 'I want to get a look at her.'

'If only she's there,' I said prayerfully.

'She'll be there,' my husband said. 'I don't see how they could hold a PTA meeting without Charles' mother.'

At the meeting I sat restlessly, scanning each comfortable matronly face, trying to determine which one hid the secret of Charles. None of them looked to me haggard enough. No-one stood up in the meeting and apologized for the way her son had been acting. No-one mentioned Charles.

After the meeting I identified and sought out Laurie's kindergarten teacher. She had a plate with a cup of tea and a piece of chocolate cake; I had a plate with a cup of tea and a piece of marshmallow cake. We manoeuvred up to one another cautiously and smiled.

'I've been so anxious to meet you,' I said. 'I'm Laurie's mother.'

'We're all so interested in Laurie,' she said.

'Well, he certainly likes kindergarten,' I said. 'He talks about it all the time.'

'We had a little trouble adjusting, the first week or so,' she said primly, 'but now he's a fine little helper. With lapses, of course.'

'Laurie usually adjusts very quickly,' I said. 'I suppose this time it's Charles' influence.'

'Charles?'

'Yes,' I said, laughing, 'you must have your hands full in that kindergarten with Charles.'

'Charles?' she said. 'We don't have any Charles in the kindergarten.'

The First Day of School

WILLIAM SAROYAN

HE WAS A little boy named Jim, the first and only child of Dr Louis Davy, 717 Mattei Building, and it was his first day at school. His father was French, a small heavy-set man of forty whose boyhood had been full of poverty and unhappiness and ambition. His mother was dead: she died when Jim was born, and the only woman he knew intimately was Amy, the Swedish housekeeper.

It was Amy who dressed him in his Sunday clothes and took him to school. Jim liked Amy, but he didn't like her for taking him to school. He told her so. All the way to school, he told her so.

I don't like you, he said.

I don't like you any more.

I like *you*, the housekeeper said.

Then why are you taking me to school? he said.

He had taken walks with Amy before, once all the way to the Court House Park for the Sunday afternoon band concert, but this walk to school was different.

What for? he said.

Everybody must go to school, the housekeeper said.

Did you go to school? he said.

No, said Amy.

Then why do I have to go? he said.

You will like it, said the housekeeper.

He walked on with her in silence, holding her hand. I don't like you, he said. I don't like you any more.

I like you, said Amy.

Then why are you taking me to school? he said again. Why?

The housekeeper knew how frightened a little boy could be about going to school.

You will like it, she said. I think you will sing songs and play games.

I don't want to, he said.

I will come and get you every afternoon, she said.

I don't like you, he told her again.

She felt very unhappy about the little boy going to school, but she knew that he would have to go.

The school building was very ugly to her and to the boy. She didn't like the way it made her feel, and going up the steps with him she wished he didn't have to go to school. The halls and rooms scared her, and him, and the smell of the place too. And he didn't like Mr Barber, the principal.

Amy despised Mr Barber.

What is the name of your son? Mr Barber said.

This is Dr Louis Davy's son, said Amy. His name is Jim. I am Dr Davy's housekeeper.

James? said Mr Barber.

Not James, said Amy, just Jim.

All right, said Mr Barber. Any middle name?

No, said Amy. He is too small for a middle name. Just Jim Davy.

All right, said Mr Barber. We'll try him out in the first grade. If he doesn't get along all right we'll try him out in kindergarten.

Dr Davy said to start him in the first grade, said Amy. Not kindergarten.

All right, said Mr Barber.

The housekeeper knew how frightened the little boy was, sitting on the chair, and she tried to let him know how much she loved him and how sorry she was about everything. She wanted to say something fine to him about everything, but she couldn't say anything, and she was very proud of the nice way he got down from the chair and stood beside Mr Barber, waiting to go with him to a classroom.

On the way home she was so proud of him she began to cry.

Miss Binney, the teacher of the first grade, was an old lady who was all dried out. The room was full of little boys and girls. School smelled strange and sad. He sat at a desk and listened carefully.

He heard some of the names: *Charles, Ernest, Alvin, Norman, Betty, Hannah, Juliet, Viola, Polly*.

He listened carefully and heard Miss Binney say, Hannah Winter, what *are* you chewing? And he saw Hannah Winter blush. He liked Hannah Winter right from the beginning.

Gum, said Hannah.

Put it in the waste-basket, said Miss Binney.

He saw the little girl walk to the front of the class, take the gum from her mouth, and drop it into the waste-basket.

And he heard Miss Binney say, Ernest Gaskin, what are *you* chewing?

Gum, said Ernest.

And he liked Ernest Gaskin too.

They met in the schoolyard, and Ernest taught him a few jokes.

Amy was in the hall when school ended. She was sullen and angry at everybody until she saw the little boy. She was amazed that he wasn't changed, that he wasn't hurt, or perhaps utterly unalive, murdered. The school and everything about it frightened her very much. She took his hand and walked out of the building with him, feeling angry and proud.

Jim said, What comes after twenty-nine?

Thirty, said Amy.

Your face is dirty, he said.

His father was very quiet at the supper table.

What comes after twenty-nine? the boy said.

Thirty, said his father.

Your face is dirty, he said.

In the morning he asked his father for a nickel.

What do you want a nickel for? his father said.

Gum, he said.

His father gave him a nickel and on the way to school he stopped at Mrs Riley's store and bought a package of Spearmint.

Do you want a piece? he asked Amy.

Do you want to give me a piece? the housekeeper said.

Jim thought about it a moment, and then he said, Yes.

Do you like me? said the housekeeper.

I like you, said Jim. Do you like me?

Yes, said the housekeeper.

Do you like school?

Jim didn't know for sure, but he knew he liked the part about the gum. And Hannah Winter. And Ernest Gaskin.

I don't know, he said.

Do you sing? asked the housekeeper.

No, we don't sing, he said.

Do you play games? she said.

Not in the school, he said. In the yard we do.

He liked the part about gum very much.

Miss Binney said, Jim Davy, what are you *chewing*?

Ha ha ha, he thought.

Gum, he said.

He walked to the waste-paper basket and back to his seat, and Hannah Winter saw him, and Ernest Gaskin too. That was the best part of school.

It began to grow too.

Ernest Gaskin, he shouted in the schoolyard, *what* are you *chewing*?

Raw elephant meat, said Ernest Gaskin. Jim Davey, what are *you* chewing?

Jim tried to think of something funny to be chewing, but he couldn't.

Gum, he said, and Ernest Gaskin laughed louder than Jim laughed when Ernest Gaskin said raw elephant meat.

It was funny no matter what you said.

Going back to the classroom Jim saw Hannah Winter in the hall.

Hannah Winter, he said, *what in the world* are you *chewing?*

The little girl was startled. She wanted to say something nice that would honestly show how nice she felt about having Jim say her name and ask her the funny question, making fun of school, but she couldn't think of anything that nice to say because they were almost in the room and there wasn't time enough.

Tutti-frutti, she said with desperate haste.

It seemed to Jim he had never before heard such a glorious word, and he kept repeating the word to himself all day.

Tutti-frutti, he said to Amy on the way home.

Amy Larson, he said, *what, are, you, chewing?*

He told his father all about it at the supper table.

He said, Once there was a hill. On the hill there was a mill. Under the mill there was a walk. Under the walk there was a key. What is it?

I don't know, his father said. What is it?

Milwaukee, said the boy.

The housekeeper was delighted.

Mill. Walk. Key, Jim said.

Tutti-frutti.

What's that? said his father.

Gum, he said. The kind Hannah Winter chews.

Who's Hannah Winter? said his father.

She's in my room, he said.

Oh, said his father.

After supper he sat on the floor with the small red and blue and yellow top that hummed while it spinned. It was all right, he guessed. It was still very sad, but the gum part of it was very funny and the Hannah Winter part very nice. Raw elephant meat, he thought with great inward delight.

Raw elephant meat, he said aloud to his father who was reading the evening paper. His father folded the paper and sat on the floor beside him.

The housekeeper saw them together on the floor and for some reason tears came to her eyes.

The Flying Machine

RAY BRADBURY

IN THE YEAR AD 400, the Emperor Yuan held his throne by the Great Wall of China, and the land was green with rain, readying itself towards the harvest, at peace, the people in his dominion neither too happy nor too sad.

Early on the morning of the first day of the first week of the second month of the new year, the Emperor Yuan was sipping tea and fanning himself against a warm breeze when a servant ran across the scarlet and blue garden tiles calling, 'Oh, Emperor, Emperor, a miracle!'

'Yes,' said the Emperor, 'the air *is* sweet this morning.'

'No, no, a miracle!' said the servant, bowing quickly.

'And this tea is good in my mouth, surely that is a miracle.'

'No, no, Your Excellency.'

'Let me guess then – the sun has risen and a new day is upon us. Or the sea is blue. That now is the finest of all miracles.'

'Excellency, a man is flying!'

'What?' The Emperor stopped his fan.

'I saw him in the air, a man flying with wings. I heard a voice call out of the sky, and when I looked up there he was, a dragon in the heavens with a man in its mouth, a dragon of paper and bamboo, coloured like the sun and the grass.'

'It is early,' said the Emperor,' and you have just wakened from a dream.'

'It is early, but I have seen what I have seen! Come, and you will see it too.'

'Sit down with me here,' said the Emperor. 'Drink some tea. It must be a strange thing, if it is true, to see a man fly. You must have time to think of it, even as I must have time to prepare myself for the sight.'

They drank tea.

'Please,' said the servant at last, 'or he will be gone.'

The Emperor rose thoughtfully. 'Now you may show me what you have seen.'

They walked into a garden, across a meadow of grass, over a small bridge, through a grove of trees, and up a tiny hill.

'There!' said the servant.

The Emperor looked into the sky.

And in the sky, flying so high that you could hardly hear him laugh, was a man; and the man was clothed in bright papers and reeds to make wings and a beautiful yellow tail, and he was soaring all about like the largest bird in a universe of birds, like a new dragon in a land of ancient dragons.

The man called down to them from high in the cool winds of morning, 'I fly, I fly!'

The servant waved to him. 'Yes, yes!'

The Emperor Yuan did not move. Instead he looked at the Great Wall of China now taking shape out of the farthest mist in the green hills, that splendid snake of stones which writhed with majesty across the entire land. That wonderful wall which had protected them for a timeless time from enemy hordes and preserved peace for years without number. He saw the town, nestled to itself by a river and a road and a hill, beginning to waken.

'Tell me,' he said to his servant, 'has anyone else seen this flying man?'

'I am the only one, Excellency,' said the servant, smiling at the sky, waving.

The Emperor watched the heavens another minute and then said, 'Call him down to me.'

'Ho, come down, come down! The Emperor wishes to see

you!' called the servant, hands cupped to his shouting mouth.

The Emperor glanced in all directions while the flying man soared down the morning wind. He saw a farmer, early in his fields, watching the sky, and he noted where the farmer stood.

The flying man alit with a rustle of paper and a creak of bamboo reeds. He came proudly to the Emperor, clumsy in his rig, at last bowing before the old man.

'What have you done?' demanded the Emperor.

'I have flown in the sky, Your Excellency,' replied the man.

'What *have* you done?' said the Emperor again.

'I have just told you!' cried the flyer.

'You have told me nothing at all.' The Emperor reached out a thin hand to touch the pretty paper and the birdlike keel of the apparatus. It smelled cool, of the wind.

'Is it not beautiful, Excellency?'

'Yes, too beautiful.'

'It is the only one in the world!' smiled the man.' And I am the inventor.'

'The *only* one in the world?'

'I swear it!'

'Who else knows of this?'

'No one. Not even my wife, who would think me mad with the sun. She thought I was making a kite. I rose in the night and walked to the cliffs far away. And when the morning breezes blew and the sun rose, I gathered my courage, Excellency, and leaped from the cliff. I flew! But my wife does not know of it.'

'Well for her, then,' said the Emperor. 'Come along.'

They walked back to the great house. The sun was full in the sky now, and the smell of the grass was refreshing. The Emperor, the servant, and the flyer paused within the huge garden.

The Emperor clapped his hands. 'Ho, guards!'

The guards came running.

'Hold this man.'

The guards seized the flyer.

'Call the executioner,' said the Emperor.

'What's this!' cried the flyer, bewildered. 'What have I done?' He began to weep, so that the beautiful paper apparatus rustled.

'Here is the man who has made a certain machine,' said the Emperor, 'and yet asks us what he has created. He does not know himself. It is only necessary that he create, without knowing why he has done so, or what this thing will do.'

The executioner came running with a sharp silver axe. He stood with his naked, large-muscled arms ready, his face covered with a serene white mask.

'One moment,' said the Emperor. He turned to a nearby table upon which sat a machine that he himself had created. The Emperor took a tiny golden key from his own neck. He fitted this key to the tiny, delicate machine and wound it up. Then he set the machine going.

The machine was a garden of metal and jewels. Set in motion, birds sang in tiny metal trees, wolves walked through miniature forests, and tiny people ran in and out of sun and shadow, fanning themselves with miniature fans, listening to the tiny emerald birds, and standing by impossibly small but tinkling fountains.

'Is it not beautiful?' said the Emperor. 'If you asked me what I have done here, I could answer you well. I have made birds sing, I have made forests murmur. I have set people to walking in this woodland, enjoying the leaves and shadows and songs. That is what I have done.'

'But, oh, Emperor!' pleaded the flyer, on his knees, the tears pouring down his face. 'I have done a similar thing! I have found beauty. I have flown on the morning wind. I have looked down on all the sleeping houses and gardens. I have smelled the sea and even *seen* it, beyond the hills, from my high place. And I have soared like a bird; oh, I cannot say how beautiful it is up there, in the sky, with the wind about me, the wind blowing me here like a feather, there like a fan, the way the sky smells in the morning! And how free one feels! *That* is beautiful too!'

'Yes,' said the Emperor sadly, 'I know it must be true. For I felt my heart move with you in the air and I wondered: what is it like? How does it feel? How do the distant pools look from so high? And how my houses and servants! Like ants? And how the distant towns not yet awake?'

'Then spare me!'

'But these are times,' said the Emperor, more sadly still, 'when one must lose a little beauty if one is to keep what little beauty one already has. I do not fear you, yourself, but I fear another man.'

'What man?'

'Some other man who, seeing you, will build a thing of bright papers and bamboo like this. But the other man will have an evil face and an evil heart, and the beauty will be gone. It is this man I fear.'

'Why? Why?'

'Who is to say that some day just such a man, in just such an apparatus of paper and reed, might not fly in the sky and drop huge stones upon the Great Wall of China?' said the Emperor.

No one moved or said a word.

'Off with his head,' said the Emperor.

The executioner whirled his silver axe.

'Burn the kite and the inventor's body and bury their ashes together,' said the Emperor.

The servants retreated to obey.

The Emperor turned to his hand-servant, who had seen the man flying. 'Hold your tongue. It was all a dream, a most sorrowful and beautiful dream. And that farmer in the distant field who also saw, tell him it would pay him to consider it only a vision. If ever the word passes around, you and the farmer die within the hour.'

'You are merciful, Emperor.'

'No, not merciful,' said the old man. Beyond the garden wall he saw the guards burning the beautiful machine of paper and reeds that smelled of the morning wind. He saw the dark smoke climb into the sky. 'No, only very much bewildered and afraid.'

He saw the guards digging a tiny pit wherein to bury the ashes. 'What is the life of one man against a million others? I must take solace from that thought.'

He took the key from its chain about his neck and once more wound up the beautiful miniature garden. He stood looking out across the land at the Great Wall, the peaceful town, the green fields, the rivers and streams. He sighed. The tiny garden whirred its hidden and delicate machinery and set itself in motion; tiny people walked in forests, tiny foxes loped through sun-speckled glades in beautiful shining pelts, and among the tiny trees flew little bits of high song and bright blue and yellow colour, flying, flying, flying in that small sky.

'Oh,' said the Emperor, closing his eyes, 'look at the birds, look at the birds!'

The Moonpath

ROBERT SWINDELLS

IF THE WORLD were flat, and if you could look straight into the rising sun, you would see the land where Nick and Bruin lived. It was a land of sticky days and breathless nights, where the sun came up like an enemy and the wind had flies in it.

At the edge of this land, where bitter waves met hot sand, there lay a town of flat, ugly buildings and narrow streets and in one of these streets stood a blacksmith's forge.

Nick was apprenticed to the blacksmith. All day in his stiff leather apron he worked by the stinging-hot furnace; pumping the bellows or carrying bars of iron for his master. At night he lay on the dusty floor with a chain on his foot. Nick's mother and father had sold him to the blacksmith for seven years. Nick cried for them sometimes, in the night, but he hated them too, and vowed they would never see him again.

Sometimes Nick's master loaded the things he had made on to a handcart, and Nick pulled it through the town to the customer's homes. As he went along, Nick would search the faces of the people he passed. He always hoped for a smile, or a kindly word, but he never found one. It was a mean, ugly town full of mean, ugly people.

One afternoon as he was hauling the cart across town he saw that a small crowd had gathered in the square. There were shouts, and some laughter. Nick left the cart and went over to look. He was small and thin, and easily slipped through to the front. In the middle of the crowd, on a small patch of beaten dust, stood a bear.

There was a collar round its neck with a chain. A man held the chain in one hand and a stick in the other. As Nick watched, the man poked the bear with the stick and cried, 'Down, Bruin!' The bear's legs collapsed and it rolled over in the dust and lay still, playing dead. The people laughed. Somebody dropped a coin in the man's hat. 'Up, Bruin!' cried the man, and he jerked on the chain. The bear clambered slowly to its feet. Nick wondered what if felt like to have a coat of thick fur on such a day as this.

The man jabbed his stick into the bear's side. 'Dance, Bruin!' he snarled.

The bear lifted its forepaws and began a slow shuffle on its hind feet, swinging its great head from side to side.

'Faster!' cried the man, and he struck the creature across its paws.

The people laughed. Bruin tried to move a little faster. There was a cloud of flies round its head; they settled near its eyes.

The man put down the stick and produced a battered mouth-organ. He sucked and blew a scratchy tune, and a few more coins fell into the hat. Bruin moved heavily to the thin music. After a while the man stopped playing and the bear dropped on to all four feet. People clapped a little. The man bowed and grinned.

Nick was turning sadly away when the bear raised its head and looked at him. The boy paused, gazing back into those tiny, pain-filled eyes. In that instant, Nick felt something that made his own eyes brim, and caused him to clamp his teeth into his bottom lip. He turned and began to push his way through the crowd. He felt the bear's eyes following him and could scarcely see through the tears in his own. He lifted the handles of his cart and went on without looking back.

That night, lying on the dusty floor with the chain on his foot, Nick thought about Bruin. He saw the fly-tortured eyes and the dry, lolling tongue and he murmured softly into the dark, 'Some day, Bruin, we will leave this place, you and I. We will sail away to a land that is white and cold as the moon. There will be no flies there, and no chains.' He moved a little and his chain made a clinking sound. He sighed, and closed his eyes. 'One day,' he murmured, and then he slept, while the cold white moon slid silent down the sky.

The next morning his master said, 'Take this boat-hook to Caspar, the fisherman. You will find him on the sand, mending his nets.'

When he stepped out of the forge the sun hit him and he screwed up his eyes. 'This land is an anvil,' he told himself. 'The sun is a great hammer, and it will beat me on the anvil until I am bent and blackened like the end of this boat-hook.' He wiped the sweat from his forehead and turned towards the sea.

Caspar was sitting cross-legged in the sand, mending a net. He looked up, squinting into the sun. 'Ah, my new boat-hook is ready, yes? Give it here.'

Nick handed it to him and stood wiggling his toes in the hot sand.

The fisherman examined the boat-hook and said, 'Tell your master I am satisfied and will pay him tomorrow.'

Nick bobbed his head, and was turning away when the man said, 'I saw you, yesterday. Watching the bear.'

Nick turned. Pale blue eyes regarding him, a twinkle in them somewhere. He nodded. 'Yes. We are both slaves, the bear and I.'

He knew he ought not to have said it. Suppose the man told his master? His eyes, fearful, met Caspar's. The twinkle remained. 'Have no fear,' said the fisherman, softy. 'I have no master, but if I had, it would have been the moonpath for me, long ago.'

Nick did not understand. 'The – moonpath?' he whispered.

Caspar nodded.

'What is the moonpath?' asked Nick. Perhaps this man was mocking him.

The fisherman raised his eyebrows. 'The moonpath? Why, the moonpath is the road to freedom; a silver track that lies upon the sea.'

Nick turned, to see warm, brown water moving slug-like in the sun. His lip twisted up. 'I see no silver track,' he said.

Caspar grinned, shaking his head. 'It is not there now, little slave,' he said. His face became grave and he patted the sand beside him. 'Come, sit here and I will tell you.'

Nick approached the man, half-fearful, and sat down. Caspar set aside his net, drew up his knees under his chin, and wrapped his thick arms around them. He gazed out over the sea.

'It is big, the sea,' he said. 'It is the biggest thing on earth, and the fiercest. To cross it you need a good boat.' He glanced sidelong at Nick. 'Slaves do not have boats. But sometimes at night, in the full of the moon, there is a way for them if they believe and are brave.'

Nick waited. After a moment, Caspar nodded towards the sea. 'Out there,' he said, 'when the moon is full, there is a path across the sea. It is long and straight, and at the far end lies a land as cool as this land is hot.' He turned earnest eyes to Nick. 'He who takes the silver path must travel quickly, for it melts with the dawn and is no more until the moon is full again.'

The boy felt a lump in his throat and he gazed at Caspar through tear-filled eyes. 'I have seen such a path,' he choked. 'It is made from light. No one can walk upon it. You mock me.'

Caspar shrugged. 'I told you. A man must believe, and be brave.' He took up a net and began to work upon it as though Nick were no longer there.

After a while the boy blinked away his tears, got up, and walked towards the town.

Many days passed. One evening, at the end of a very hard day, Nick's master beat him and left him waterless. Nick lay a long time crying in the dust. When he had cried all his tears, he sat up and rubbed his eyes with the heels of his hands so that the dust from them made a grey paste on his cheeks.

'I will not stay here,' he told himself, 'to be beaten and starved and roasted. I will run away. I will go tonight.' And he crawled across the floor to where his master had left a large file. His chain was barely long enough, but by lying at full stretch he was able to get his finger-tips to it. He laid the blade across a link and, working rapidly, began to saw at the iron.

An hour he worked, then rested, gasping. He blinked away the sweat and went on. At midnight the link parted. Nick scrambled to his feet and stood, listening. The moon-washed streets were silent.

He left the forge on tiptoe, flitting from shadow to shadow along the road. He did not know where he would go. The town was surrounded on three sides by the desert, and on the other by the sea. The desert, then. He must try to cross the desert. He turned up an alley, and cried out in terror. His master came swiftly, crouching, the great hammer drawn back over a brawny shoulder. Nick whirled and fled.

'Runaway!' roared his master behind him.

His voice echoed all across the midnight town. A door was flung open. Then another. Lights moved in windows. People spilled out of houses. Nick swerved and ran on. The people were shouting to one another. His way was blocked. He spun round. Men, strung out across the street behind him, and his master like some squat ape coming with the hammer. He ran left. A figure crouched, spreading huge arms. He spun. There! A clear run. He gasped, pelting along the unguarded alley, and as he ran he cried out, without knowing it, the name of the only other slave he knew. 'Bruin! Bruin! Bruin! . . .'

Breaking clear of the buildings he glanced over his shoulder. His master followed, closer now, his hammer raised high. Nick ran on desperately then stopped, skidding in damp sand. The sea! They had driven him to the sea! He turned, sobbing, and angled along the beach, dodging between huge rocks and leaping over small ones. He could hear the pounding of his master's boots and the rasping of his breath. He threw back his head and ran wild-eyed, mouth agape. He never saw the rock. It struck him below the knees and he went headlong in the sand. He rolled and screamed, flinging up his arms to cover his face. His master raised the great hammer. A cry. The hammer fell, kicking up sand by Nick's head, and then his master reeled, clutching his side.

A shaggy form swayed erect against the moon, snarling. Bruin! The bear turned, a short length of chain swinging at its neck. Nick gazed up at the great head and then beyond, to where the moon hung cool and full in the velvet sky. Cool and full. Caspar! The boy looked seaward, and it was there. 'I believe!' sobbed Nick.

Men were coming, running quiet in the sand. He scrambled to his feet. 'Come, Bruin!' he cried.

The sand sloped gently down, and they ran; not into surf, but on to rippled silver, cool and hard. 'I believe!' cried Nick, and they moved out across the midnight sea.

And all along the shore the people stood, their mouths open, staring. One stuck out his foot and snatched it back, drenched with moon-white spray. So they stood, all night, gazing out to sea. From time to time someone would shake his head, or mutter something under his breath. And when it was near to dawn, they looked at one another out of the corners of their eyes, and shuffled their feet, and began to drift away in ones and twos. They walked by the blacksmith, who nursed his side by a rock. And the blacksmith said to one, 'Where is my boy?', and to another, 'What happened?' But they just shook their heads like people in a dream.

And then the bear's master came dangling the broken lock from Bruin's cage. Far, far away, a cooling wind ruffled Nick's hair and Bruin dropped his head to lap the snow.

The Wind between the Stars

MARGARET MAHY

ONE DAY WHEN Phoebe was small, her old Granny came in shaking
her head and saying, 'The wind's blowing from right between the
stars tonight.' Little Phoebe stopped playing and listened to the
wind. It sounded big enough to snatch up the hills in its right hand
and the moon in its left, and to carry them away for always.

'From right between the stars?' Phoebe asked.

'Three times around the world and off again,' said her Granny.
'Off between the stars – and if anyone wants to go with it, it will
take them – yes – but they mustn't hope to come back again.
That's the way of the wind from between the stars.'

Phoebe lay in her bed and listened to that wind. She thought she
heard pattering feet and laughter, and tears and singing and fingers
scratching at the window.

'Shall I open my window,' thought little Phoebe, 'in case the
wind doesn't ever blow from between the stars again?'

Her bed was warm and she was sleepy. Betwixt the beginning
and the end of her thought she fell asleep, and the wind from
between the stars blew around the world three times and went off
again without her.

Phoebe grew up to be a young girl with wild black hair and long
dancing legs. She ran like a hare over the springtime hills, racing
the wind that blew in from the sea. She laughed to feel the new
grass under her bare feet, and to smell the scents of the sea and
earth the wind carried with it. At her side ran Michael, her
friend, strong and brown as a tree, nimble as a goat.

'I've never been so happy,' said Phoebe, laughing and looking at the world through the net of her own tangled hair. 'We've raced the wind, Michael, we've left it behind.'

'I can hear it coming after us,' Michael said. 'Listen!'

Far away Phoebe heard the wind murmuring and saw the trees bend before it. Suddenly it changed. Its note grew deeper and stronger. It boomed like a solemn drum, and yet it piped a high music, shrill and clear.

'It's singing!' Phoebe called. 'It's singing.' She heard the laughter and the tears and the pattering feet. But Michael took her hand and started to run down the hill, pulling her after him. 'Why,' said Phoebe, 'it's that wind back again – the wind from between the stars. Stop, Michael, stop and listen, Michael.'

Michael would not stop. 'It's not a usual sort of wind,' he cried. 'It may mean trouble. It's best to be inside when it comes.'

Phoebe ran with him, half willing, half sorry. Before the door of her grandmother's cottage shut her safely in, she peeped back over her shoulder and saw, in a somersault second, the wind whirling a few leaves down the street behind her. It sang its huge song, and Phoebe thought she saw – just perhaps – a whole crowd of people streaming and dancing down the street, people so strange she thought she must have dreamed them in the dark blink of an eye.

The wind blew and sang three times around the world and then was off, out between the stars again.

Phoebe stayed behind. She married Michael and they had six children and a happy life together. Slowly her wild black hair was tamed – at last it was all held down with net and pins – it began to turn white. Slowly her long legs forgot how to dance and Phoebe hid them under petticoats, a skirt and an apron. Her children grew up and went away and one day Michael died, an old man. Phoebe was all alone. She did not have much money so she went to work for Miss Gibb who lived in a tall, white house a mile out of the village.

Miss Gibb matched her house. She was tall and cold and white. No wild flowers or unruly grass grew around Miss Gibb's house, and there were no wild flowers or untidy corners in her heart either. She lived alone with the hundred beautiful dresses she had worn when she was young. She did not wear them now but she thought of them, she took them down and looked at them or stroked them as they hung in their long rows.

'Do you remember?' she whispered – and the silk whispered back, 'Remember, remember.'

Phoebe had never met anyone as cold and white and tall as Miss Gibb. Doing just whatever Miss Gibb told her to do, she scuttled around like a frightened little mouse not daring to talk, or smile, or even to look at Miss Gibb, while Miss Gibb always looked over Phoebe's head as if she was staring into some ruined garden or a world where it is always winter.

One day Miss Gibb smelled honeysuckle and mignonette in the air. She decided her dresses would like to be out in the sun and told Phoebe to take them down from their wardrobe and hang them on the line. There was not room on the line. Phoebe hung most of them under the trees, where they swayed like big flowers, like great bunches of bright fruit. Miss Gibb's neat garden blossomed out in a strange summer of silk and velvet, lace, chiffon, muslin, taffeta and satin. The whole garden murmured and sighed, waking to rustling life as the breeze moved among the dresses.

Phoebe went into Miss Gibb's room to bring out the last dresses. She put them over her arm and was about to carry them out into the garden when suddenly she saw her reflection in the mirror opposite. Phoebe hadn't seen herself in such a fine mirror for a long time, and she stopped, amazed. Who was that little withered creature shuffling along, white-haired and faded? What had happened to Phoebe, the little girl dancing in front of the winter fire, or to long-legged Phoebe dancing over the hills, watching the world through a net of black hair? A net of wrinkles sat over Phoebe's face now and she had forgotten how to dance.

'Yet,' thought Phoebe, 'I don't feel so different. I'm still the same. Here I am. Here I am. But who is there to remember me? Who is there left to call me by my name, "Phoebe", to know who I really am, and to see the real me looking out from behind all these wrinkles?' A thought came to her, 'I wonder if I can still dance?'

Phoebe tucked her petticoats up a bit and began to dance. Stiff and old as they were, Phoebe's feet remembered their dancing. They fell happily into the old gay steps and Phoebe danced, still light on her toes, like a tune on a squeaky penny whistle, or a little spiral of dust lifting in the summer wind.

'See,' said Phoebe to the old Phoebe in the glass, 'I'm still there!' She turned on her toes and nearly banged into Miss Gibb standing stone-still, icicle-cold, in the doorway.

'Really Mrs Moffat,' said Miss Gibb, using Phoebe's other name and speaking in a small, chilly voice. 'Do you have to do your prancing here all over my carpet in front of my mirror?' Poor Phoebe felt lost.

'Nobody knows me,' she thought. 'They only know that little old woman in the mirror – and this isn't so surprising, because that's who I really am.'

'I'm sorry, miss,' she said to Miss Gibb. 'I don't know what came over me.'

'Make sure it doesn't come over you again,' Miss Gibb said. 'And for goodness sake, be careful of my dresses.'

Phoebe looked at Miss Gibb and suddenly saw that Miss Gibb, too, spent long times in front of her mirror, staring bewildered, wondering what had happened to the girl who had worn those hundred beautiful dresses, who had once been loved and admired.

'This getting old, miss,' said Phoebe, 'it's a terrible hard thing but it comes to everyone.'

Miss Gibb looked over Phoebe's head, out of the window into the sunny garden, but her eyes reflected a winter that wasn't really there. 'Do the work you are paid to do Mrs Moffat, and don't chatter.' Out in the garden the dresses suddenly moved on the trees and a deeper murmur was heard stirring and growing.

'The wind!' Miss Gibb said. 'How annoying! Bring my dresses in at once, Mrs Moffat.' But Phoebe stood quite still and listened.

'The wind!' she said. 'The wind from between the stars.'

It came over the house like a great wave and the dresses under the trees broke free, and soared and swirled around, high up around the chimney, curtseying, and bowing, mopping and mowing, in the air. They seemed worn by unseen, laughing people.

'Shut the window!' screamed Miss Gibb. 'The wind will take us all!'

'Open the window,' said Phoebe. 'The wind can take me if it wants to, along with all its other dead leaves.'

'Mrs Moffat, close the window!' said Miss Gibb. But Phoebe was beyond all fearing. All she could feel was happiness – someone knew her, someone had remembered her, someone knew what she really was, and had called to remind her.

'Miss Gibb, don't be scared, Miss Gibb,' Phoebe called. She flung the window open and the wind filled the whole house. It rang with sounds of laughter and song and carried with it the company of people it had collected around the world, and in and out of the stars. Kings crowned with ears of corn and crimson poppies, peacocks, mermaids, comets, the twelve dancing princesses, dragonflies, Helen of Troy, lyre birds, minstrels with lutes, gypsies to tell your fortune, little silver fish, frogs and roses, Rapunzel, wound around in her own shining hair, the crippled lizard-beggarman from near Alpha Centauri. There were laughing lions, their manes plaited with flowers, centaurs, and vast shadowy people with wings. Some faces smiled and some wept, as all these people wandered and wavered, melted and moved on the huge breath of the wind. Dancing among them went Miss Gibb's hundred dresses, but whether they were worn by unseen wind people or just tossed by the wind, who can say?

'Oh,' cried Phoebe, 'here I am. Here I am!'

'Well, we've waited long enough for you,' said a lion. 'Twice we've come looking for you, but you always wanted to do something else. Now take your feet off the ground and come too.'

Phoebe laughed breathlessly. 'May I? Can I?'

'Try,' said a king, sighing past her, smelling of autumn and of sun shining on ripe corn. Phoebe stepped, danced, and then in her dance lifted her feet off the ground. Slowly the wind took her, turned her over upside down, around, around . . . Phoebe squeaked like a little mouse, 'Oh! Oh! I'm upside down!'

'It's a wonderful way to see the world,' said a princess, hanging head down beside her, tapping her worn dancing shoes on the ceiling before she slowly turned head over heels softly down, and her place was taken by a row of Miss Gibb's dancing dresses – the pink foaming bubbling organza, the sleek black velvet, the tender shimmering silk looking like silver tears. They bowed to Phoebe, but she could only wave back, for it was her turn to slide down the lap of the wind to bob and laugh with the shy mermaids, to hold in her hands for a moment the scaly paw of the lizard-beggar, to vanish in a swirling spiral of leaves and rose petals.

'Going . . .' said the wind. 'We're going . . . we can't wait.'

'But Miss Gibb,' Phoebe said. 'Let Miss Gibb come too.'

'Take your feet of the ground, Miss Gibb,' called the lions and the mermaids. No, Miss Gibb could not take her feet from the ground. She could only stare and snatch at her dancing dresses.

But the wind, the wind from between the stars, took them as it takes all things that flow and are free. Carrying Phoebe on its back, riding her along like a queen in triumph, it swept three times around the world and off out between the stars once more . . . and if anyone wants to go with it, it will take them, but they mustn't hope to come back again.

Court Martial

CHARLES C. O'CONNELL

HE STOOD PALLID and tense before the officers. Though he was now unarmed and shorn of all his field equipment, his tunic seemed to drag heavily on his shoulders, and the weight of his helmet was almost unbearable; he could hardly keep his head erect. His right arm, which had been twisted viciously behind his back, hung limply by his side, numb and lifeless, except for the faint pulse that beat under his arm-pit.

He stood with his feet apart, although years of discipline urged him to stand to attention, but he knew that if he did so he would topple over. In fact, it made no difference how he presented himself; the verdict of the court martial would be 'guilty'. He had disobeyed orders. Only his own conscience could justify his action. According to their code, he was a rebel . . . Well, let it be. If he had to relive the episode, he would do exactly the same thing.

The heat inside was quite intolerable. He longed to step back a little into the current of air that moved the canvas by the door, yet he dared not. Such an action might antagonize his judges even more, and although he could see no vestige of mercy or even humanity in their stern faces, he had hope that perhaps, in spite of everything, they would understand.

'You have heard the evidence.' The voice of his superior officer jarred on his ears. 'Have you anything to say?'

The prisoner thought for a moment. Had he anything to say in his defence? No, he had not — nothing that they could understand.

But what could he not say of this useless bloodshed, which was for assassins rather than soldiers! This war on women and innocent children was repugnant to him. Nothing, he thought, could justify this mass murder, yet to say so here would be treason.

'Answer!' snarled the officer.

'I have nothing to say.'

'Do you deny that you allowed those refugees through?'

Perhaps it would be better if he said something – anything to shorten the farcical trial. 'I let them through,' he said hoarsely, admitting the charge for the first time.

The officer smiled. 'Against your specific orders?'

'Yes.'

Why in the name of glory did they persist in this mockery?

The two officers held a whispered consultation. One of the guards behind the prisoner shuffled for an instant and was still again. Then the second officer spoke. His was a soft face with none of the harsh lines of his superior, but his eyes were colder than a winter dawn.

'We should be interested to know why you allowed all three to go. Had you done your duty by one, there would have been no further trouble. Were they friends of yours? Did you know them? Or were you tempted by the amount of the bribe?'

The prisoner shook his head, and the perspiration temporarily held by his eyebrows trickled to his chin. 'They offered no bribe, sir. I did not know them.'

'Then why did you let them through?'

'I thought it was – just.'

'What do you know of justice?' the officer sneered.

The prisoner closed his eyes. Once again the picture of those three weary travellers came to his mind. They were fleeing from a terror which he represented. He had not harmed them because they looked so desperately tired, or perhaps it had been that heart-searching appeal in the young woman's eyes, or perhaps it was because of the child, so helpless in a world gone mad . . .

Whatever the reason, his orders had suddenly appeared monstrously evil.

He opened his eyes. 'I am a soldier,' he said firmly. 'I will not become an assassin.'

And then the guard behind him struck him at the base of the neck and he slumped to the ground. He was vaguely conscious of being kicked, but it did not hurt any more. A strange sense of unreality possessed him, as though he existed only in a dream.

Some time later, he found himself on his feet again. The business of the court had finished. There had been no death sentence. One of the officers merely nodded his head to the guard, and the prisoner was propelled towards the door.

He staggered as he came into the sunlight, and his helmet fell off. Nobody picked it up – he would have no further use for it. The cool air stirring through his matted hair was as invigorating as wine. He was rushed forward and then, some paces from the door behind a high, screening boulder, his guards stopped.

The prisoner was under no illusion. He knew that in a few moments he would be dead. Yet he had no regrets. Perhaps it would be better to leave this world of injustice and suffering.

Vaguely, he wondered if it would always be like this. That could hardly be possible. Men must one day realize the futility of bloodshed. Perhaps, in a thousand or two thousand years, men would have at last learnt to live in peace and there would be no greed, nor wars, nor murder.

He stood erect. He did not feel afraid. He was filled with a strange, new hope. He thought of those three travel-stained refugees. He hoped they got through to Egypt. Once there, the child would be safe from Herod's barbarous assassins . . .

The Children of Grupp

PENELOPE LIVELY

WHEN TREVOR CARTWRIGHT first saw the Medusa fountain it was
the nymphs which caught his attention. Naturally enough. He set
down the wheelbarrow for a moment and had a good look; very
nice too, all those luscious marble girls. It was his second day as
trainee gardener at Rockwell Manor under the Youth Opportunities
Programme. He was seventeen; he'd rather have been elsewhere;
he wanted farm work, proper stuff with machinery, not messing
about manicuring hedges and sweeping up leaves.

The gardens of Rockwell Manor are renowned for topiary and
statues. The Medusa fountain, at the end of the famous Yew Walk,
is of course the *pièce de resistance*. The Medusa, framed by ferns and
the dripping grotto, presides over the great basin of the fountain,
at the base of which a charming group of cherubs is arranged in
frozen play. Around the rim of the basin sit or recline youthful
naked figures – exquisite Apollos and the languid nymphs which
appealed to Trevor. The Medusa herself is so encrusted with moss
and lichen that she is barely recognizable as a face, while the
snakes of her hair have long since fused with the background of
rock and greenery. Trevor did not even see her, on that first
occasion; in any case he did not like to hang around too long or
he'd have Fletcher down on him like a ton of bricks. Fletcher was
the head gardener, and a right so-and-so. That he was in fact a first
cousin once removed of Trevor's did not qualify his brusque
treatment of the newest YOP. So, having taken in the girls and the

blokes and all those stone babies larking around in the cool green water – no bad place to be, on a sweltering August afternoon – Trevor upended the wheelbarrow once more and set off towards his next task.

He knew the gardens well enough, of course. He'd been born and grown up a mile away. The hamlet of Grupp, a dour little collection of tied cottages, has traditionally supplied the labour force for the Manor and its gardens, open to the public since the nineteen thirties. Trevor's grandfather had worked there, and his great-grandfather before that. His own father had managed to break out, and got himself into the building trade when times were better. Now, the economic climate had forced Trevor back into the mould; resentfully, he had presented himself at the estate office. His mother, of a more subservient and less querulous generation, had told him off for being truculent: 'There's always been a to and fro between Grupp and the Manor. They're funny people, the Saxbys, but they done all right by the village. Back in Grandad's day there was estate parties once a year – swimming in the fountain, for the children, and a skittle alley in the stable yard.' Trevor was unimpressed.

The present owner, Colonel Saxby, was a recluse, inflated by local rumour to a vaguely sinister figure, for no reliable reason. The wider world certainly found him unaccommodating; art historians interested in the statuary were turned away with a handout to the effect that no records existed concerning the provenance of the various pieces and that photography was not allowed. The figures were of indeterminate age – most appeared to be vaguely eighteenth century, though some of the draped classical ladies presiding over the Yew Walk might well have been earlier. The Medusa fountain was a puzzle – those experts who had been able to inspect it closely felt that as a group it was not consistent: figures seemed to have been added at different times. Even the cherubs – the adorable children tumbling and laughing around the foot of the

fountain itself – appeared to the practised eye to be slightly at odds
with one another, some so worn by time that features and dimples
had almost vanished, others with their smiles and marble curls
still sharply sculptured.

The gardens did not, in fact, attract large numbers of visitors.
Advertising was desultory; opening times were capricious. Of
those who did come, most were struck by the melancholy
atmosphere of the place, an atmosphere that seemed indeed to
spill out into the surrounding countryside, so that the dark
hedgerows and lowering copses became an extension of the
brooding woodland and sombre rides of the Manor gardens. Those
who knew no better said that a few good herbaceous borders
would have cheered the place up; others, more practised in
earlier traditions of gardening, commented on its picturesque
qualities but still felt a chill as they plodded down endless vistas
between dank hedges from which stared the blank stone eyes of
Dianas and Cupids and Apollos. If, on leaving the car park, they
failed to take the turn that led back to the main road and fetched
up by mistake in Grupp, the sense of gloom and abandonment
would be reinforced. The cottages had a sullen look; there was
neither shop nor pub. Appearance, indeed, was reinforced by
reputation; Grupp people were said to keep themselves to
themselves, there was gossip about inbreeding and absence of
initiative. Certainly, the hamlet had today a semi-abandoned air;
several of the cottages were in derelict condition. Aspiring
purchasers from Birmingham or London were turned away at the
estate office with a blunt refusal: estate cottages were never put on
the market. A demographic historian, attracted by interestingly
high infant mortality rates, was met with cold stares and slammed
front doors.

Trevor, a child of Grupp, knew only that he yearned for a proper
man's job with machinery – tractors and muck-spreaders and
combines – instead of which here he was stuck in the gardens with

a wheelbarrow and a rake and Fletcher bawling him out if he deviated from instructions for an instant. He found himself working in isolation for the most part, hand-weeding on his knees in remoter regions of the gardens, monotonously raking lawns, trundling barrowloads of debris to the compost heaps. It was a summer of relentless heat and humidity. Employees at Rockwell were required to dress decorously. On his first day Trevor had stripped to the waist, and was roundly abused by Fletcher; thereafter he sweated in his shirt and cast envious glances at the marble nudity all round him – the gleaming torsos, the pale curves of buttocks and breasts, the slender bared limbs. It was all a bit sexy, too, no question about it, could get you quite worked up when you were on your own with them – waving their arses at you from among the trees.

After his first brief glimpse of the Medusa fountain Trevor found himself irresistibly drawn to the spot. He made several illicit detours that way, for the pleasure of a quick splash of the face and hands in the water. There was something gloomy about the place, that was undeniable, but the watery cool of it, and the silver splash of the fountain, compensated for the gloom, while he came to feel the figures positively companionable. One particular nymph became a favourite. There she sat, curled on the rim of the basin with her hand held shyly over her breasts, as though she had been caught out in a private skinny-dip. On first acquaintance he had found her arousing; now, after several visits, he looked at her differently, seeing her beautiful immobility as in some way sad and vulnerable. She seemed to have an expression of eternal shock and surprise in her blank stone eyes; there was a quality in her face that was familiar, too. To be honest, she had a look of his Auntie Marian. Even, ever so slightly, of his own mum.

He became bolder in his visits to the fountain. He lingered for longer, trailed his hands and arms in the water, sat on the rim of the basin for a minute or two, idly splashing. He was tempting providence, and providence, inevitably, struck. He had dunked his face in the water and was vigorously sousing his hair when a voice made him spring guiltily upright. 'Take a dip then, boy. Go on. Get stripped off. No need to be ashamed of your body – you'd stand comparison with that lot, by the look of you!'

It was the Colonel. Couldn't be anyone else. There he stood, just below the Medusa head – short, stocky, tweed-suited, grinning from the ferns and rocks of the grotto. Creepy, sprung from nowhere like that.

'We're not allowed to,' stammered Trevor. 'We're not allowed to take us shirts off, even.'

'It'll be between you and me,' said the Colonel. 'Who's to know? Old Fletcher's busy in the greenhouses. You can take your time. Go on, boy – don't be a fool.' He bared his teeth at Trevor in what was apparently meant as a smile, and was gone. No wonder people said he was a peculiar old bastard.

Trevor looked around. It was quite true – Fletcher was occupied elsewhere. It was not a public opening day. He was quite alone. He hesitated, then ripped off his shirt, jeans and underpants and stepped into the fountain.

It was wonderful. Deliciously cool, and deeper than you would have thought. He was up to his waist. He waded around, revelling in it. He swam a few strokes. Then he rolled on his back and floated, blissfully, gazing up at the dappled ceiling of leaves that flickered across a pale blue sky. He could have stayed there for ever.

Wiser to cut short the risk, though. Better get going. Reluctantly, he stood up, stepped to the edge, hauled himself out onto the rim and sat with his legs in the water to savour a last few delightful moments. The stone figures around him mirrored the contours of his own pink young body. He glanced, a touch complacently, at his lean torso, his flat muscular flanks, his long legs; what had the old bloke said about comparisons with that lot?

He looked across the pool at the grotto; the Medusa, snake-haired and mossy, stared straight at him. The light seemed to dim, as though the sun had gone in; the frolicking cherubs dulled from gold to grey. It wasn't so warm, either; he started to withdraw his legs from the water. They felt oddly stiff and leaden; maybe he'd got a bit of a cramp. He sat, trying to flex his toes; he seemed to have no sensation in them at all. He could see them, down there in the greenish water, as though they were someone else's.

He reached out for his shirt, lying on the barrow behind him, to give himself a rub down with it. At least, he tried to reach – but now his arm too was numb, leaden, he could scarcely lift it. He hauled it an inch or two – and it fell back inert in his lap. Panic seized him: I'm ill! he thought. I've had a heart attack, like Grandad – I'll die, sat here like this. He tried to shout, and his jaw would not move. He dragged his hand up to his face, with hideous effort; he touched his mouth, saw his fist lie against it, and felt nothing.

He moved his head, inch by inch, fighting his own rigidity; he tried to look towards the great Yew Walk, to see if anyone might be within sight. He could not see that far, but he was looking now at his neighbour on the rim of the fountain, at the nymph, the girl, his favourite, she who shielded her breasts with one hand in eternal modesty. And her stone eyes met his, it seemed, not in shock or surprise but in terrible grief.

He saw the colour ebb from his own body. He saw the delicate veining of marble appear on his thighs. He saw himself become uniform with the nymphs, with Apollo, with the mermaid and the satyr and with the cherubs – those plump children frozen in play at the foot of the fountain, their marble curls touched with golden lichen. Some while after all feeling had left him, when he knew himself to be no longer a creature of flesh and blood but an object deep within which there lurked some awful consciousness of what had once been – sometime then he heard and saw the Colonel. He saw him come again and stand below the grotto, contemplating his possessions. But Trevor had lost all sense of time by then; it might have been the next day, or the next month or the next year. Time would cease to be for Trevor: the seasons would succeed one another as he remained locked within the prison of his fine young body. The snow would lie in ridges along his arms, heap up on his thighs and fill his lap. The summer sun would bake him. The autumn leaves would pile up around him and float on to the surface of the water. He would hear the voices of visitors, the blank globes of his eyes would register their passage – bright moving blurs of colour beyond the rigid presences of his companions, suspended in time, locked in a dreadful eternity of weather and memory. There they would sit and recline, the handsome youths, the graceful girls. And the cherubs . . . Oh, but the thought of the children of Grupp is beyond bearing.

Little Black Pies

JOHN GORDON

'GHOSTS,' SHE SAID. 'There ain't no such thing.'

Emma Stittle watched her plump arm spread and become fatter as she pressed it on the kitchen table.

'There ain't no such thing,' she repeated, and with her thumb stripped peas from a pod, cupped them in the palm of her hand and raised them to her mouth. 'Ghosts is a load of old squit.'

Her sister Sarah, thinner and older, rattled the poker between the bars of the kitchen stove, and red coals and ashes fell into the grate. 'It get so hot in this kitchen on a summer's day,' she said, 'that I wonder I bother to cook anything at all.'

'Me,' said Emma, 'I reckon it's stupid to think that people who eat can die and then turn into somethin' that don't need food.' She chewed as she slit another pod with her thumbnail. 'I like peas, but there ain't no substance in 'em.'

Sarah had no time to talk of ghosts. 'I'm that hot I don't know what to do with myself,' she said as she hobbled towards the cottage door, narrow-shouldered and stooping. She lifted the latch and pulled the door open. 'Come you on in then,' she said. 'All on you, you little black devils.' A great ramp of sunlight streamed through the door to brighten the tile floor. 'Flies,' she said, 'swarms on 'em.'

There was a dance of black specks above Emma's head but she paid no heed. 'When our old mother used to talk of ghosts,' she said, 'she used to make me frit. She used to say they come back because their time weren't properly run. That there was unfinished business or somethin' like that. Load of old squit.'

'Who does all the work round here? Who?' Sarah, like her sister, wore a flowered, wrap around apron, and both had their hair drawn back into buns, but Sarah's hair was grey while her sister's was still glossy black. 'I scrimp and save and slave and scrub,' she said, coming back to the table, 'and what thanks did I ever get for it? She died, didn't she? And never no word of thanks. Not one.' She banged an earthenware bowl on to the bare wood of the table in front of Emma and began scooping flour into it from a big jar.

Emma sat where she was, her round cheeks dimpling as she munched. 'You look a bit wore up today, Sarah,' she said. 'What's been gettin' you down, gal?'

Sarah cut a wedge of lard and began rubbing it into the flour with her skinny brown fingers. 'I slaved all o' them years after Father died and Mother was left alone. I skivvied from morning till night and what help did I get?' She dug savagely into the white mess.

'I were much younger than you, Sarah, don't forget. Only a little kid when Mother were taken poorly. And I used to sit beside her up in her room and keep her company hour after hour.'

Sarah did not look her way. Her blue eyes, fading with age, gazed at where her fingers dug. 'Spoilt brat.' The wrinkles of her thin face arranged themselves into a simper and her voice took on an acid whine. 'Please, Sarah, Mummy's sent me down for a cup of tea. I'll take it up, Sarah. Mummy don't want nobody else to disturb her.'

'I weren't ever as bad as that. You're putting it on.' Emma was laughing. 'But she did like me to sit with her. She used to sit in that old high-backed chair by the window, with her shawl around her, and her pillows, and I used to pull aside the lace curtain so as we could see down into the lane, and she used to tell me things about everybody that came by.' Emma chewed and laughed again. 'She told me things no kid ought never to have been told. About women in the village. And men.'

Sarah paid her no attention. She poured a little water from a jug into the basin and mixed it in with a knife, jabbing. 'Best frock. Always best frock because, ''Mummy like to see me pretty.'' And who done the scrubbing with a sack tied round her waist? Who took out the ashes and blackleaded the stove? Twice a week I done that, and all the cracks in the skin o' me fingers shown up like black spider webs.'

But Emma was in a reverie. She gazed through the open door across the lane to where the yew trees shaped themselves against the blue sky. 'She used to love a funeral. Especially if they dug the grave near enough so she could see the coffin go down. She used to love telling me how people died. Little Claudie Copp called for his Mum all through one night, she say, and he never once see her alongside his bed. And then in the morning, Mother used to say, he went up to heaven with the angels.'

'Like black spider webs.' Sarah slashed the dough across and lifted half of it on to a piece of oilcloth where she had sprinkled flour. 'I could've had nice hands. Nice soft white hands like I seen some girls have, but they was always in water. Always scrubbing.'

'It was lucky for her we lived just across from the churchyard,' said Emma. 'Gave her an interest. People always visitin' graveyards. And stayin' there in the end.' She laughed again and looked towards her sister, but Sarah had a new grievance.

'I could've had him if I wasn't so thin and dry and wore out with work. I could've.' She rubbed flour on to the rolling pin and began to roll out the dough. 'I had his child, didn't I?' The pastry was a thin white island on the oilcloth. 'I had his little baby.' A tear came from the inner corner of one faded eye, but was so thin it did no more than moisten the side of her nose.

'You never did!' Emma's eyes gleamed with surprise and curiosity. 'Whose baby? You never said nothing. I never seen no baby.'

Sarah had turned her back to get a pie dish from the window

ledge. 'I never told nobody. Nobody ever knew.'

'But who was he, Sarah? I never knew you had a feller.' Her sister remained silent, and Emma became sly. 'I don't mean you never had admirers. I used to think my Tom looked at you a bit. Used to, till I made him stop.'

Sarah lifted the pastry and began to line the pie dish. 'Tom were a lovely man.' The glisten of a tear came and went. 'He were lovely.'

'So I were right.' Emma turned her plump face away and patted the glossy bun at the back of her head. 'I guessed as much. Tom never said nothing but I guessed as much.'

'If I'd told him about the child he would have married me. I know that. But I could never hold a man because of that — not when his eyes was on my own sister.'

Emma had jerked towards her, her mouth open, but Sarah's voice did not change its pitch.

'So I lost him, didn't I?' She had lifted the pie dish and was trimming the pastry at the edge. 'And there was nothing but the baby.'

'Tom's baby.' Emma's whisper was as soft as the ash that fell in the grate.

'It died,' said Sarah. 'I made it die. And it lies yonder still, under that tree. No father, no mother, nothing.'

Emma's round face was pinched suddenly and her voice was harsh and vindictive. 'It's as well for you there ain't no such thing as ghosts, Sarah Stittle, or else you would be haunted!'

But Sarah spoke as though Emma was not there. 'First she took Mother from me, then she took Tom, and I never said a word. Never said, and I ought to have done. I ought to have said.'

Emma opened her mouth to speak, but a sudden flutter of wings in the doorway made both sisters start. A jackdaw, twisting his grey nape in the sunshine, stood on the step.

Emma gasped. 'My God, that were like the angel o' death. That whole doorway seemed full of black wings. I can't stand birds. I hate them stiff feathers. Go away! Get out, you devil of hell!'

But Sarah was wiping her hands on her apron as she went towards the doorway. Her face softened with pleasure. 'Come on then, my beauty. Come you on in and see your Auntie Sarie. There now, there now.' She stooped and held out a finger. The bird hopped on it. 'Lovely little cold black claws you've got, my lovely boy. Hold tight to your auntie.'

'Take it away! Take it away!' Emma shrank back in her chair. 'Please, Sarah!'

But Sarah spoke only to the bird. 'You came when I needed you, my lovely. You came hopping over the road just when I were down in the dumps, my lovely boy.' She raised the bird and her dry lips touched his black bill.

'Sarah! I can't bear it!'

'Just when I needed you, you came hopping along with your black eye. And didn't you know it all, didn't you just know it?' For the first time, the bird against her cheek, its black feathers touching her grey hair, she looked directly towards her sister. 'Emma took my man, didn't she? Emma took my man. But you showed me, didn't you, boy? You showed me how he'd never have her. Never no more. Skippety along the lane, skippety down the hollow. You showed me the pretty flower and the little black berry. The little black berry I put in the pie. One, two, three . . . many, many more. In a little pie for Emma. Emma's little pie.'

'You're talking daft, Sarah. What you on about? Throw that bird out. Get rid of it.'

'And Emma never knew.' Sarah sat and stroked the bird, looking no more towards her sister. 'Emma never knew about them little black berries what she ate. Ate many and many a time.'

'My stomach,' said Emma. 'I had a bad stomach and you gave me little pies to ease it. They was nice.' She tried to smile, but although the dimples came they were pale.

'I gave her pies, my beauty. Little black pies. And now she ain't got no stomach-ache no more. Nothing no more.'

Emma made herself laugh. 'Sarah!' she called. 'Sarah, look at me!' But Sarah did not stir. 'Sarah, you make me feel bad. What did you do to me?'

Sarah held the bird so her nose was touching its deep grey cap. 'I wish we could tell her what we done, Jack my beauty. I wish we could tell her, but it's too late now.'

'What do you mean too late? What you done to me?'

But Sarah ignored her sister's cry, kissed the bird and put it down on the table. 'You like to peck peas, Jack. There you are, my little boy, my lovey. Go you peck them peas.'

The fat woman pressed her arm on the table and clenched her fist on the peas.

'You ain't going to scare me,' she said. 'You ain't going to scare me with your talk. You talk as if I was dead. But if I was, how come I'm here?' She laughed, defying her sister. 'There ain't no such thing as ghosts.'

The bird's black claws skittered on the table top as it went towards the clenched fist. Emma clutched tight, refusing to move. The bird stabbed down. She clutched tighter and shrieked. But the room was silent. And the black beak pecked through a hand that nobody but Emma herself could see.

Paths

JOHN CHRISTOPHER

HAVING DECIDED TO take a long way home through the fields, he found it easy to talk himself into the still longer route through the wood. When he had been little he had thought wild animals lived in it: wolves and bears. Later he heard tales of its being haunted. He didn't believe them, but even at eleven he could frighten himself at night by imagining being taken somehow from his bed and finding himself alone there. A summer afternoon was different, though.

Before entering the wood, he looked back. The new junior school from which he had just come lay in bright sunlight; it glittered especially from the solar panels on the south side of the tower. The panels extended outwards from the top, giving it a weird shape. The tower looked a bit like a bird with half-folded wings, getting ready to fly.

Trees crowded close. Usually there was birdsong, but today it was very quiet. All he heard were his footsteps on the soft earth, the occasional crackle of a twig. He came to the place, roughly at the wood's centre, where there was a grassy mound, three or four metres across. The path skirted the mound, and normally the clearing would have been sunlit; surprisingly, the tree tops were lost in a mist. Two more things surprised him. Other paths he had never seen led into the clearing; and there was a girl sitting on the mound.

She wore funny clothes, and a lot of them: a white dress, white stockings, laced-up white boots. The dress was buttoned to the neck, with long sleeves and starched cuffs, and reached nearly to her ankles. She had long dark hair under a straw hat with blue ribbons. Her face was pale, eyes brown. Her nose was a bit long. She wouldn't have been pretty, he decided, even in normal clothes.

Going towards her, he asked: 'What's all this, then – fancy dress?'

She paused before answering. 'Who are you?' Her voice was light but sharp, and very precise. 'Are you a farmer's boy?'

She must be crackers: how could he be a farm worker, at his age?

'I'm Kevin Luscombe. I live in Southleigh. What's your name?'

She hesitated again. 'Arabella Cartwright. Where, in Southleigh?'

'Cherrytree Road.'

She shook her head. 'There's no such place. Only London Road and Dover Road, and the Green.'

She spoke like someone describing a village. Those were all streets in the old part of the town: the Green was the main shopping centre.

She was staring at him suspiciously. 'What's that, written across your jersey?'

He glanced down at his T-shirt. 'You can read, can't you?'

'It says: "The Tripods are Coming". What does it mean?'

'It's a new TV serial – science fiction. My dad knows one of the cameramen.'

She said doubtfully: 'Science fiction? Teevy? Camera men?'

He looked at her dress again, remembering something else from television – about Victorian children living near a railway line. Feeling a bit foolish, he said: 'What year is it?'

'Don't be silly!'

'Go on. Tell me. What year?'

'Eighteen eighty-four. You know that.'

'No,' he said, 'I don't. And it isn't. It's nineteen. Nineteen eighty-four.'

They sat on the mound and talked, and came to a kind of understanding. If you thought of time as a spinning wheel, with the years as spokes, this was the hub. There was no way of knowing how or why each had got here. The wood had been spoken of in her time, Arabella said, as a magic place: the mound was said to hide a ruin from ancient times.

They were curious about each other's worlds; she more so, since while he knew something about hers from history, his was totally unknown to her. He spoke of flying machines, radio and television. She said wistfully: 'I'd love to see some of it.'

He looked at her. 'Why not? Which path did you come by?' She pointed. 'That one's mine. I can take you along it, to my time.'

She said no at first – scared, he guessed. He kept on; she wavered, and eventually agreed. But as they slid off the mound, they saw someone approaching along one of the other paths.

It was a boy about their age, dressed in a tight-fitting green tunic with a padded front reaching to mid thigh. Puffed sleeves were slashed at elbow and shoulder to show a crimson shirt underneath. It looked like silk, as did the striped red and yellow stockings which covered his legs down to soft leather boots. He wore a pointed hat, with feathers at the back. He stopped when he saw them, and muttered something.

Kevin asked him: 'What year are you from?'

'Who art tha?'

It sounded part fearful, part angry. Kevin tried to explain, but he did not seem to understand.

'Who art tha?', he repeated. 'Frenchies? Spaniards, mayhap? 'Tis certain tha'rt not English.'

'Of course we're English!'

They both tried quizzing him, but did not get far. His accent was thick, Irish-sounding. Suddenly he said: 'My horse.' It sounded like 'hairse'. 'She's not well tethered. I mun see to it.'

He turned and went back along the path, almost running. Kevin said: 'From what time, do you think? Elizabethan?'

'His clothes would suggest it. And when I mentioned Mary Queen of Scots, he called her 'that traitress', as though she were

alive still. I was reading about her lately: she was beheaded in
fifteen eighty-seven.'

'So he could be from fifteen eighty-four?'

'Yes, I would think so.'

'Then what about seventeen eighty-four, or sixteen eighty-four?'

'They may still come. Or perhaps no one went into the wood in
those years.'

He shrugged. 'Anyway, I was taking you to nineteen eighty-four.'

She followed silently, obviously nervous. He reached the edge
of the wood and stopped to let her come up with him; then saw she
had stopped, too, a couple of metres back. In a low voice, she said:
'No.'

'There's nothing to be frightened of. We don't need to go into
the town. You can look at things from a distance.'

'No. I'm sorry.'

She turned back, and he followed. She was a girl, of course; he
ought not to be surprised at timidness being stronger than curiosity.

When they got back to the mound, a boy was there: younger
and smaller than the one in Elizabethan finery, and looking little
better than a savage. He wore a smock of coarse grey cloth,
roughly stitched with twine, and nothing else. His hair was
tousled; arms, legs and feet thickly grimed. A bare sole of foot
looked like a pad of black leather. He was playing with a pebble,
and clenched it inside his fist when he saw them.

They tried questioning him, too, but with even less success. He
spoke in a growling inarticulate voice. Kevin asked Arabella: 'Did
you understand any of that?'

'A word, here and there. I'm sure he said ''wood''. Isn't that
an old English word?'

'Is it?'

'He might be Saxon.'

From 984, Kevin wondered. Or 884? Wouldn't that be about
the time Alfred the Great was trying to hold back the Danes?

He said: 'I don't fancy going along his path, whenever he's from.'

Arabella shivered. 'No, indeed.'

'On the other hand, I wouldn't mind taking a look into *your* time.'
She smiled. It was a nice smile; her nose wasn't really long.
'I'd like to show you.'

As he followed her, it occurred to him that they had no idea
how long the wood might stay open to travellers from the
different centuries. What if it closed up, and he was forced to stay
in 1884? Well, he would miss his parents, sister, friends at school.
On the other hand, it would certainly be exciting! And if he could
remember details of one or two important inventions of the past
hundred years, he might become famous, rich . . .

The shock hit him without warning as the trees thinned to show
open space ahead: it brought sharp fear, a sickness in the stomach.
He tried to force his way forward and managed a couple of steps,
but no more. He was shivering.

Arabella turned round. 'What is it, Kevin?' She looked at him.
'You can't either, can you?'

He made an effort which brought sweat to his brow, and shook
his head.

She said quietly: 'I wondered. I thought perhaps it wasn't just
me. We can't get into any year except our own.'

He felt defeated and ashamed. 'I suppose we'd better go back,
to the mound.'

'You must, to find your path.' Her voice was low. 'This is mine.'

'We can . . . talk.'

'We have talked.' She managed a shadowy smile. 'I'm glad we
met.'

He said: 'Don't go yet!'

She came towards him, and he thought she had changed her
mind. But all she did was lean forward and briefly kiss him. The
straw hat was harsh against his skin, but her lips were soft.

'Goodbye, Kevin.'

In the field beyond the wood a man with a plough followed two horses. He watched her out of sight, but she didn't look back. He walked down the path, wondering what would happen to her, and corrected himself: what *had* happened. There was no way of knowing – or was there? The old churchyard at the back of the Green . . . She could have moved away from Southleigh, of course, but she might not. It wasn't likely to be Arabella Cartwright; she would probably have married. But there weren't that many Arabellas, and he knew her year of birth. 'RIP Arabella — , born 1873, beloved wife of . . .' He let the thought go. He knew he wasn't going to look for that gravestone.

The clearing was empty, but he saw the savage boy on one of the paths, returning to whatever barbarous home he had come from. At least Arabella had gone back to a solid, comfortable world. Without TV or video, cars or aeroplanes or computers, but a hopeful world; good in itself and with better things to come. He and she had that in common.

He wondered about the savage boy's world. He had no temptation to go into it, even if that were possible, but it would do no harm to look. There might be knights riding across the hillside, or Vikings – Roman soldiers, even.

He followed, and caught sight of him again as he reached the edge of the wood. Just as the boy stepped into the open, he dropped the pebble he had been playing with. Kevin fought the same feeling of resistance and sickness as he walked the last few metres. He picked up the pebble and called out, but the boy walked on, unhearing. He walked across an empty untilled field: no knights, Vikings, Roman soldiers. No buildings, either.

Apart from a ruin of some sort, in the distance. It was overgrown, shapeless except for one bit that stood out. Ivy trailed from a shattered tower. The outline was blurred, yet he could still recognize it. A bird with a half-folded wing, getting ready to fly . . . long broken and abandoned.

Kevin looked at the pebble he had picked up. It wasn't a pebble, in fact, but a thin square of battered metal, with a panel of crazed plastic let in one side. Behind that it was just possible to make out the face of a digital watch.

He let it drop and ran down the path, heading for home.

The Aliens

ROGER MALISSON

'HOW MANY OF them are there going to be, Dad?' Terri asked, a little nervously.

'Oh, only two.' His father, Ambassador to the United Galactic Federation of Planets, tried to make his voice sound confident and reassuring.

Terri felt his mother shiver slightly. She was sitting beside him in the transit capsule as it sped along the gleaming tunnels beneath the city of Norica. Terri could sense that both his parents were rather scared about the forthcoming ordeal.

Norica was the main city of the Planet Thuron, and it held the giant Ambassadorial Centre to which every intelligent, space-travelling race in the Galaxy sent representatives. Terri's father was one of these.

New candidates to join the Federation of Planets were very rare. In fact, for centuries past, there had been none. Then suddenly an alien ship had appeared in the skies over Norica. Excitement everywhere had been intense, and the Joint Council of the Federation of Planets had immediately sent up a party of officials to interview the newcomers.

And what newcomers! Everything about them was supposed to be top-secret, but certain details had leaked out. They were an entirely alien species of people, quite unlike any ever seen before; monsters, some said. Terri felt himself growing worried at the prospect of actually seeing them in the flesh. He had begged and persuaded his parents to be taken along when he first heard that his father had been invited to the official presentation of the Aliens to the Joint Council. Now he was not so sure that he really wanted to see them for himself. His classmate Edda, daughter of the Menian Ambassador, claimed that they were too horrible to look at. Supposing they really were that dreadful . . .?

'Do you think we should have brought Terri, dear?' his mother asked anxiously. 'Isn't he a little too young?'

'Of course I'm not,' Terri interrupted scornfully, before his father had a chance to reply. 'I'm not scared of what they'll look like, Mother. Anyhow, I'm going to be an Ambassador myself one day. You have to learn to deal with all sorts of creatures.'

'That's right.' His father glanced at Terri approvingly, pressing the buttons that guided the capsule into the right tunnel. 'You can't judge any species by looks alone. Maybe they are a little weird to our way of thinking. But they've passed the first test of an advanced race; they've made it into space and reached all the way from their home planet to Thuron. So we must assume that, appearances apart, they are as civilised as we are.'

His wife was not convinced.

'Well, I hope they are as civilised as you say,' she said. 'But don't forget, they must be well behind us in space travel or it wouldn't have taken them this long to find out about Thuron. When you really think about it,' she added, 'they're practically primitives. I bet it isn't many years since they were living in caves, or whatever they have on their planet.'

It was a disturbing thought.

'But think of the Martians,' Terri argued. 'They look like huge insects and I expect everybody was frightened of them when they first arrived. But they're a perfectly reasonable race, and everyone's so used to them now that we hardly notice all those legs and feelers they have.'

'Exactly,' nodded his father. 'It's the same with the Radians. Just imagine what a shock you'd have if you saw a Radian for the first time! Two heads, all that fur, and the way they hop about

instead of walking is very strange when you think about it. Yet
they're generally considered to be the wisest race in the whole
Galactic Federation.'

'I expect you're right,' said Terri's mother reluctantly.
'Anyway, we haven't even seen these Aliens yet. They may look
quite normal.'

Their capsule was docking smoothly now in the area beneath
the Assembly Building, and Terri peered eagerly out of the
window to see the other Ambassadors disembarking. Most of
them had arrived separately and entered the Assembly Hall by
their own private escalators, since they each needed different
environments and air supplies.

'What sort of atmosphere do the Aliens need, Dad?' he asked as
his father climbed out of the capsule.

'I don't know, but it gave the Federation Technicians a lot of
headaches to prepare it. They breathe a rather strange gas mixture.'

'Gas . . .?' Terri's mother's voice was faint, but full of foreboding.

'It's all right, dear,' the Ambassador said patiently as he helped
her up the ramp and into the escalator which would take them into
their own pressurised observation-booth. 'They will be kept quite
separate from the rest of us. They aren't properly out of
quarantine yet.'

Perhaps the Aliens had brought some dreadful plague with
them, thought Terri, his flesh creeping. Or suppose they were
violent? They might smash their way out of their observation-booth
and run amok. He began to wonder if he could pretend a
stomach-ache and be sent back – but then, Edda would laugh at
him and tease him for being a scaredy-cat. He had boasted to the
whole class when his father had told him that he had permission to
go to the Presentation. Nobody else had been able to attend.
Everybody had been so jealous, and Terri had felt really proud.

But what if he panicked when he saw the Aliens? Suppose they
were as terrifying as Edda said, so ugly and repulsive that you
would wake up screaming every night for a month afterwards if

you even glimpsed one once?

'I may have hysterics,' his mother was saying in a very calm voice as she seated herself in the booth. 'If these Creatures are as bad as I have heard, I shan't answer for the consequences when I see them.'

His father gave her a cross look.

'Really, dear, you should try to be a little more broad-minded if only for Terri's sake,' he said. 'You'll frighten him with your silly talk. I tell you they're not horrible to look at. They are probably very pleasant Creatures.'

Terri's mother sniffed, unconvinced. 'Just as long as they behave. What is that ghastly mess spread out on the table down there?'

Terri adjusted the viewing screen in front of them so that it scanned in close-up across the area where the Reception Committee was gathered, waiting to greet the Aliens formally.

'Food,' his father said shortly.

'Food?' Terri and his mother exchanged horrified looks. 'That – sickening heap of rotting garbage? Do you mean they *eat* that?' His mother's voice had risen an octave.

'Apparently. The Federation Corps is very accurate when it comes to duplicating these things.'

Terri thought that even his father did not sound too sure; as for himself, his stomach turned over at the disgusting sight. A lot of sickening, chopped-up dead creatures and different kinds of plants, most of it partly burned for some reason, was spread out on the table below. Whatever could the Aliens be like, to eat such a foul-looking mess?

He suddenly became aware that all the lights in the vast Hall were dimming, except for those in the Reception Booth. All the Ambassadors craned forwards for their first glimpses of the Aliens. Voices died away into silence, and then through the speaker Terri heard the president of the Council begin his address of welcome.

His mouth dried and he tensed up completely as the door at the rear of the Hall slowly opened. A brilliant light danced down to illuminate the Aliens emerging through it. Please, please, Terri thought desperately, don't let me make a fool of myself. Don't let me scream . . .

The Aliens came into the light. They were certainly odd – one was pink, and one was brown, and they only had two flat eyes each at the front of their round heads; but they were not as awful as all that.

Terri shot his mother a look of relief, and slowly relaxed. He was already imagining what he would say to Edda in class tomorrow, something really offhand and casual:

'Oh, they're OK, Edda, they don't frighten me. Earthmen? I can take 'em or leave 'em.'

And Terri settled back into his chair, comfortably coiling his seven tentacles beneath him.

The Star Beast

NICHOLAS STUART GRAY

SOON UPON A time, and not so far ahead, there was a long streak of light down the night sky, a flicker of fire, and a terrible bang that startled all who heard it, even those who were normally inured to noise. When day came, the matter was discussed, argued, and finally dismissed. For no one could discover any cause at all for the disturbance.

Shortly afterwards, at a farm, there was heard a scrabbling at the door, and a crying. When the people went to see what was there, they found a creature. It was not easy to tell what sort of creature, but far too easy to tell that it was hurt and hungry and afraid. Only its pain and hunger had brought it to the door for help.

Being used to beasts, the farmer and his wife tended the thing. They put it in a loose-box and tended it. They brought water in a big basin and it drank thirstily, but with some difficulty – for it seemed to want to lift it to its mouth instead of lapping, and the basin was too big, and it was too weak. So it lapped. The farmer dressed the great burn that seared its thigh and shoulder and arm. He was kind enough, in a rough way, but the creature moaned, and set its teeth, and muttered strange sounds, and clenched its front paws . . .

Those front paws . . .! They were so like human hands that it was quite startling to see them. Even with their soft covering of grey fur they were slender, long-fingered, with the fine nails of a girl. And its body was like that of a boy – a half-grown lad – though it was as tall as a man. Its head was man-shaped. The long and slanting eyes were as yellow as topaz, and shone from inside with their own light. And the lashes were thick and silvery.

'It's a monkey of some kind,' decided the farmer.

'But so beautiful,' said his wife. 'I've never heard of a monkey like this. They're charming – pretty – amusing – all in their own way. But not beautiful, as a real person might be.'

They were concerned when the creature refused to eat. It turned away its furry face, with those wonderful eyes, the straight nose, and curving fine lips, and would not touch the best of the season's hay. It would not touch the dog biscuits or the bones. Even the boiled cod-head that was meant for the cats' supper, it refused. In the end, it settled for milk. It lapped it delicately out of the big basin, making small movements of its hands – its forepaws – as though it would have preferred some smaller utensil that it could lift to its mouth.

Word went round. People came to look at the strange and injured creature in the barn. Many people came. From the village, the town, and the city. They prodded it, and examined it, turning it this way and that. But no one could decide just what it was. A beast for sure. A monkey, most likely. Escaped from a circus or menagerie. Yet whoever had lost it made no attempt to retrieve it, made no offer of reward for its return.

Its injuries healed. The soft fur grew again over the bare grey skin. Experts from the city came and took it away for more detailed examination. The wife of the farmer was sad to see it go. She had grown quite attached to it.

'It was getting to know me,' said she. 'And it talked to me – in its fashion.'

The farmer nodded slowly and thoughtfully.

'It was odd,' he said, 'the way it would imitate what one said. You know, like a parrot does. Not real talking, of course, just imitation.'

'Of course,' said his wife. 'I never thought it was real talk. I'm not so silly.'

It was good at imitating speech, the creature. Very soon, it had learned many words and phrases, and began to string them together quite quickly, and with surprising sense. One might have thought it knew what it meant – if one was silly.

The professors and elders and priests who now took the creature in hand were far from silly. They were puzzled, and amused, and interested – at first. They looked at it, in the disused monkey-cage at the city's menagerie, where it was kept. And it stood upright, on finely-furred feet as arched and perfect as the feet of an ancient statue.

'It is oddly human,' said the learned men.

They amused themselves by bringing it a chair and watching it sit down gracefully, though not very comfortably, as if it was used to furniture of better shape and construction. They gave it a plate and a cup, and it ate with its hands most daintily, looking round as though for some sort of cutlery. But it was not thought safe to trust it with a knife.

'It is only a beast,' said everyone. 'However clever at imitation.'

'It's so quick to learn,' said some.

'But not in any way human.'

'No,' said the creature, 'I am not human. But, in my own place, I am a man.'

'Parrot-talk!' laughed the elders, uneasily.

The professors of living and dead languages taught it simple speech.

After a week, it said to them:

'I understand all the words you use. They are very easy. And you cannot quite express what you mean, in any of your tongues. A child of my race – ' It stopped, for it had no wish to seem impolite, and then it said, 'There is a language that is spoken throughout the universe. If you will allow me – '

And softly and musically it began to utter a babble of meaningless nonsense at which all the professors laughed loudly.

'Parrot-talk!' they jeered. 'Pretty Polly! Pretty Polly!'

For they were much annoyed. And they mocked the creature

into cowering silence.

The professors of logic came to the same conclusions as the others.

'Your logic is at fault,' the creature had told them, despairingly. 'I have disproved your conclusions again and again. You will not listen or try to understand.'

'Who could understand parrot-talk?'

'I am no parrot, but a man in my own place. Define a man. I walk upright. I think. I collate facts. I imagine. I anticipate. I learn. I speak. What is a man by your definition?'

'Pretty Polly!' said the professors.

They were very angry. One of them hit the creature with his walking-cane. No one likes to be set on a level with a beast. And the beast covered its face with its hands, and was silent.

It was warier when the mathematicians came. It added two and two together for them. They were amazed. It subtracted eight from ten. They wondered at it. It divided twenty by five. They marvelled. It took courage. It said:

'But you have reached a point where your formulae and calculuses fail. There is a simple law – one by which you reached the earth long ago – one by which you can leave it at will – '

The professors were furious.

'Parrot! Parrot!' they shouted.

'No! In my own place – '

The beast fell silent.

Then came the priests, smiling kindly – except to one another. For with each other they argued furiously and loathingly regarding their own views on rule and theory.

'Oh, stop!' said the creature, pleadingly.

It lifted its hands towards them and its golden eyes were full of pity.

'You make everything petty and meaningless,' it said. 'Let me tell you of the Master-Plan of the Universe. It is so simple and nothing to do with gods or rules, myths or superstition. Nothing to do with fear.'

The priests were so outraged that they forgot to hate one another. They screamed wildly with one voice:

'Wicked!'

They fled from the creature, jamming in the cage door in their haste to escape and forget the soul-less, evil thing. And the beast sighed and hid its sorrowful face, and took refuge in increasing silence.

The elders grew to hate it. They disliked the imitating and the parrot-talk, the golden eyes, the sorrow, the pity. They took away its chair, its table, its plate and cup. They ordered it to walk properly – on all fours, like any other beast.

'But in my own place – '

It broke off there. Yet some sort of pride, or stubbornness, or courage, made it refuse to crawl, no matter what they threatened or did.

They sold it to a circus.

A small sum was sent to the farmer who had first found the thing, and the rest of its price went into the state coffers for making weapons for a pending war.

The man who owned the circus was not especially brutal, as such men go. He was used to training beasts, for he was himself the chief attraction of the show, with his lions and tigers, half-drugged and toothless as they were. He said it was no use being too easy on animals.

'They don't understand over-kindness,' said he. 'They get to despising you. You have to show who's master.'

He showed the creature who was master.

He made it jump through hoops and do simple sums on a blackboard. At first it also tried to speak to the people who came to look at it. It would say, in its soft and bell-clear tones:

'Oh, listen – I can tell you things – '

Everyone was amazed at its cleverness and most entertained by the eager way it spoke. And such parrot-nonsense it talked!

'Hark at it!' they cried. 'It wants to tell us things, bless it!'

'About the other side of the moon!'

'The far side of Saturn!'

'Who taught it to say all this stuff?'

'It's saying something about the block in mathematics now!'

'And the language of infinity!'

'Logic!'

'And the Master-Plan!'

They rolled about, helpess with laughter in their ringside seats.

It was even more entertaining to watch the creature doing its sums on the big blackboard, which two attendants would turn so that everyone could admire the cleverness: 2 and 2, and the beautifully-formed 4 that it wrote beneath. $10 - 8 = 2$. Five into 20. 11 from 12.

'How clever it is,' said a small girl, admiringly.

Her father smiled.

'It's the trainer who's clever,' he said. 'The animal knows nothing of what it does. Only what it has been taught. By kindness, of course,' he added quickly, as the child looked sad.

'Oh, good,' said she, brightening. 'I wouldn't like it hurt. It's so sweet.'

But even she had to laugh when it came to the hoop-jumping. For the creature hated doing it. And, although the long whip of the trainer never actually touched its grey fur, yet it cowered at the cracking sound. Surprising, if anyone had wondered why. And it ran, upright on its fine furred feet, and graceful in spite of the red and yellow clothes it was wearing, and it jumped through the hoops. And then more hoops were brought. And these were surrounded by inflammable material and set on fire. The audience was enthralled. For the beast was terrified of fire, for some reason. It would shrink back and clutch at its shoulder, its arm, its thigh. It would stare up wildly into the roof of the great circus canopy — as if it could see through it and out to the sky beyond — as though it sought desperately for help that would not come. And it shook and trembled. And the whip cracked. And it cried aloud as it came to each flaming hoop. But it jumped.

And it stopped talking to the people. Sometimes it would almost speak, but then it would give a hunted glance towards the ring-master, and lapse into silence. Yet always it walked and ran and jumped as a man would do these things – upright. Not on all fours, like a proper beast.

And soon a particularly dangerous tightrope dance took the fancy of the people. The beast was sold to a small touring animal-show. It was getting very poor in entertainment value, anyway. It moved sluggishly. Its fur was draggled and dull. It had even stopped screaming at the fiery hoops. And – it was such an eerie, man-like thing to have around. Everyone was glad to see it go.

In the dreary little show where it went, no one even pretended to understand animals. They just showed them in their cages. Their small, fetid cages. To begin with, the keeper would bring the strange creature out to perform for the onlookers. But it was a boring performance. Whip or no whip, hunger or less hunger, the beast could no longer run or jump properly. It shambled round and round, dull-eyed and silent. People merely wondered what sort of animal it was, but not with any great interest. It could hardly even be made to flinch at fire, not even when sparks touched its fur. It was sold to a collector of rare beasts. And he took it to his little menagerie on the edge of his estate near a forest.

He was not really very interested in his creatures. It was a passing hobby for a very rich man. Something to talk about among his friends. Only once he came to inspect his new acquisition. He prodded it with a stick. He thought it rather an ugly, dreary animal.

'I heard that you used to talk, parrot-fashion,' said he. 'Go on, then, say something.'

It only cowered. He prodded it some more.

'I read about you when they had you in the city,' said the man, prodding harder. 'You used to talk, I know you did. So talk now. You used to say all sorts of clever things. That you were a man in your own place. Go on, tell me you're a man.'

'Pretty Polly,' mumbled the creature, almost inaudibly.

Nothing would make it speak again.

It was so boring that no one took much notice or care of it. And one night it escaped from its cage.

The last glimpse that anyone saw of it was by a hunter in the deeps of the forest.

It was going slowly looking in terror at rabbits and squirrels. It was weeping aloud and trying desperately to walk on all fours.

Breakfast

JOHN STEINBECK

THIS THING FILLS me with pleasure. I don't know why, I can see it in the smallest detail. I find myself recalling it again and again, each time bringing more detail out of a sunken memory, remembering brings the curious warm pleasure.

It was very early in the morning. The eastern mountains were black-blue, but behind them the light stood up faintly coloured at the mountain rims with a washed red, growing colder, greyer and darker as it went up and overhead until, at a place near the west, it merged with pure night.

And it was cold, not painfully so, but cold enough so that I rubbed my hands and shoved them deep into my pockets and I hunched my shoulders up and scuffled my feet on the ground. Down in the valley where I was, the earth was that lavender grey of dawn. I walked along a country road and ahead of me I saw a tent that was only a little lighter grey than the ground. Beside the tent there was a flash of orange fire seeping out of the cracks of an old rusty iron stove. Grey smoke spurted up out of the stubby stovepipe, spurted up a long way before it spread out and dissipated.

I saw a young woman beside the stove, really a girl. She was dressed in a faded cotton skirt and waist. As I came close I saw that she carried a baby in a crooked arm and the baby was nursing, its head under her waist out of the cold. The mother moved about, poking the fire, shifting the rusty lids of the stove to make a greater draught, opening the oven door; and all the time the baby was nursing, but that didn't interfere with the mother's work, nor with the light quick gracefulness of her movements. There was something very precise and practised in her movements. The orange fire flicked out of the cracks in the stove and threw dancing reflections on the tent.

I was close now and I could smell frying bacon and baking bread, the warmest, pleasantest odours I know. From the east the light grew swiftly. I came near to the stove and stretched my hands out to it and shivered all over when the warmth struck me. Then the tent-flap jerked up and a young man came out and an older man followed him. They were dressed in new blue dungarees and in new dungaree coats with the brass buttons shining. They were sharp-faced men, and they looked much alike.

The younger had a dark stubble beard and the older had a grey stubble beard. Their heads and faces were wet, their hair dripped with water, and water stood out on their stiff beards and their cheeks shone with water. Together they stood looking quietly at the lightening east; they yawned together and looked at the light on the hill rims. They turned and saw me.

''Morning,' said the older man. His face was neither friendly nor unfriendly.

''Morning, sir,' I said.

''Morning,' said the young man.

The water was slowly drying on their faces. They came to the stove and warmed their hands at it.

The girl kept to her work, her face averted and her eyes on what she was doing. Her hair was tied back out of her eyes with a string and it hung down her back and swayed as she worked. She set tin cups on a big packing-box, set tin plates and knives and forks out too. Then she scooped fried bacon out of the deep grease and laid it on a big tin platter, and the bacon cricked and rustled as it grew crisp. She opened the rusty oven door and took out a square pan full of high big biscuits.

When the smell of that hot bread came out, both of the men inhaled deeply. The young man said softly: 'Keerist!'

The elder man turned to me: 'Had your breakfast?'

'No.'

'Well, sit down with us, then.'

That was the signal. We went to the packing-case and squatted on the ground about it. The young man asked: 'Picking cotton?'

'No.'

'We had twelve days' work so far,' the young man said.

The girl spoke from the stove. 'They even got new clothes.'

The two men looked down at their new dungarees and they both smiled a little.

The girl set out the platter of bacon, the brown high biscuits, a bowl of bacon gravy and a pot of coffee, and then she squatted down by the box too. The baby was still nursing, its head up under her waist out of the cold. I could hear the sucking noises it made.

We filled our plates, poured bacon gravy over our biscuits and sugared our coffee. The older man filled his mouth full and he chewed and chewed and swallowed. Then he said: 'God Almighty, it's good,' and he filled his mouth again.

The young man said: 'We been eating good for twelve days.'

We all ate quickly, frantically, and refilled our plates and ate quickly again until we were full and warm. The hot bitter coffee scalded our throats. We threw the last little bit with the grounds in it on the earth and refilled our cups.

There was colour in the light now, a reddish gleam that made the air seem colder. The two men faced the east and their faces were lighted by the dawn, and I looked up for a moment and saw the image of the mountain and the light coming over it reflected in the older man's eyes.

Then the two men threw the grounds from their cups on the earth and they stood up together. 'Got to get going,' the older man said.

The younger turned to me. ''Fyou want to pick cotton, we could maybe get you on.'

'No. I got to go along. Thanks for breakfast.'

The older man waved his hand in a negative. 'OK. Glad to have you.' They walked away together. The air was blazing with light at the eastern skyline. And I walked away down the country road.

That's all. I know, of course, some of the reasons why it was pleasant. But there was some element of great beauty there that makes the rush of warmth when I think of it.

Acknowledgements

Thanks are due to the following for permission to reproduce stories: p. 1 'The Pudding Like a Night on the Sea' by Ann Cameron from *The Julian Stories*, © Ann Cameron, 1981, reproduced by permission of Victor Gollancz; p.16 'M13 on Form' by Gene Kemp from *Hundreds and Hundreds*, reproduced by permission of Laurence Pollinger Limited; p.42 'Nothing to be Afraid of' by Jan Mark, reproduced by permission of Penguin Books Limited; p.50 'The Poison Ladies' by H.E. Bates from *The Watercress Girl and Other Stories*, reproduced by permission of Laurence Pollinger Limited and the Estate of H.E. Bates; p.58 'Smart Ice Cream' by Paul Jennings from *Unreal*, reproduced by permission of Penguin Books Australia Limited; p.67 'Wolf Alone' by Jan Needle from *The Methuen Book of Animal Tales* published by Methuen Children's Books, reproduced by permission of Reed Consumer Books Limited; p. 73 'The Banana Tree' by James Berry, reproduced by permission of Penguin Books Limited; p. 82 'Charles' by Shirley Jackson from *The Lottery*, reproduced by permission of Farrar, Straus and Co. Inc. © 1948/9; p. 88 'The First Day of School' by William Saroyan from *Best Stories of William Saroyan*, reproduced by permission of Laurence Pollinger Limited and The William Saroyan Foundation; p. 94 'The Flying Machine' by Ray Bradbury from *S is for Space*, reproduced by permission of the Peters Fraser & Dunlop Group Limited; p. 106 'The Wind between the Stars' by Margaret Mahy from *The Door in the Air*, reproduced by permission of J.M. Dent & Sons Limited; p. 115 'The Children of Grupp' by Penelope Lively, © Penelope Lively, 1988, reproduced by permission of Murray Pollinger; p. 122 'Little Black Pies' by John Gordon from *Catch Your Death*, reproduced by permission of The Lutterworth Press, James Clark & Co., Limited; p. 128 'Paths' by John Christopher © John Christopher; p.148 'Breakfast' by John Steinbeck from *The Long Valley* published by William Heinemann Limited, reproduced by permission of Reed Consumer Books Limited.

Every attempt has been made to locate copyright holders for all material in this book. The publishers would be glad to hear from anyone whose copyright has been unwittingly infringed.